BEYOND BOLD

BEYOND BOLD

INSPIRATION/COLLABORATION/EVOLUTION
SHEILA BRADY/LISA DELPLACE/ERIC GROFT
OEHME, VAN SWEDEN | OvS
TEXT BY TOM CHRISTOPHER

POINTED LEAF PRESS

4

5

6

"The friendship that began on that cold morning, when Jim's warmth filled the room, has grown and continued over the past decade, as project after project has come online at the Botanic Garden. Now when Chicago Botanic Garden visitors look out toward Evening Island, they see a classic 'New American Garden' landscape. What I see is the face of a friend, whose smile and sparkling eyes said it all on that morning we first met, and whose gifts have continued to delight and instruct literally hundreds of thousands of visitors each year since then. 'Nothing short of FABULOUS,' as Jim would say."
—Barbara Whitney Carr, August 2010

The story goes on. James van Sweden would see to that. In 2009, Jim was focused on *sustainability*.

Having been diagnosed with Parkinson's disease several years earlier, Jim was preoccupied with the health and continuity of the business that he and Wolfgang Oehme founded in 1975. Rather than keep the succession planning just among colleagues and friends, he shared the lessons learned about the transition process with the profession. In August of that year, he wrote in *Landscape Architecture Magazine*:

"SUSTAINABILITY. The other day, I realized that despite our constant use of the term to describe best practices, we designers seldom think about how sustainability applies to the continued existence of our firms."

Jim asked pointedly:

"What if next month comes and you aren't there to sign the checks? Will the life of your firm end when you die or retire, or will another generation of partners chart a course for the future?"

Wolfgang passed away in December of 2011, and Jim in 2013. Planning for the future, however, was well under way, with Jim serving as the guardian, curator, and matchmaker safeguarding the OvS legacy.

With Wolfgang's retirement in 2008 and Jim's just three years later, the baton was passed to Sheila Brady, Eric Groft, and Lisa Delplace, who had all joined the firm between 1986 and 1988. These three Next Generation principals, whose work is showcased in *Beyond Bold*, represent a combined commitment of more than a century of mentorship and leadership that began during the founders' tenure and continues to this day. When the three joined the then-tiny practice— following professional experiences in larger offices, and fortified with their landscape architecture degrees from Harvard's Graduate School of Design [Brady], van Sweden's alma mater, the University of Michigan [Delplace], and the University of Virginia [Groft]—the emerging professionals entered a unique boutique practice that was ascendant. Jim and Wolfgang had already made their mark on residential design (their August 1985 article in the *New York Times* about Alex and Carole

Rosenberg's garden amped up the buzz), and they garnered enviable publicity for their innovative work on the garden at the Federal Reserve Board in Washington, DC—a project that has been ongoing in the office since 1977. The founding partners recognized that an opportunity for an expanded geographic and typological portfolio was at hand.

Lisa Delplace remembers that this was an exciting period, one when Jim would frequently broadcast, "We're really rolling now." With a burgeoning project list and growing staff, the aspirational principals moved the office from its humble location atop a Georgetown dress shop (which could accommodate up to five employees) to a roomy Beaux Arts former bank building on Capitol Hill that the two purchased in 1987. To this day, whenever I set foot into the OvS office, that bold burnt-orange color of the walls hits me with a welcome punch—just like the fall color that infuses an OvS garden.

Sheila Brady said of Wolfgang that he "nurtured [us in] how to make our gardens green…. He taught us all how to work with soils, how to work with plants both native and non-native, and [how to choose] plants that are vigorous, take off, and that are drought tolerant. We were inducted into that. Those words were not even part of the vocabulary. It was just a process. So, this whole evolution of green is innate to us. It comes out in all our work."

Jim believed he and Wolfgang had a responsibility as mentors who should never "miss the opportunity to play a role in cultivating staff members' knowledge and taste." Jim encouraged travel and photography as ways to see, problem-solve, and remember. He viewed the office as a "salon" with "fabulous" guests invited in to educate, enlighten, and entertain. There are great stories of visits by Roberto Burle Marx, Penelope Hobhouse, and Martha Schwartz. Everything was curated: the food and wine, the art that hung on the walls, as well as the patrons/ clients who came by and became close friends, travelling companions, and ambassadors for the practice. This approach to design was as much a part of the OvS legacy as the gardens and landscapes the firm planned and built. John D. Rockefeller, one of the greatest landscape patrons ever, who virtually kept the Olmsted Brothers' practice afloat during the Great Depression, once said: "A friendship founded on business is better than a business founded on friendship."

The OvS approach to practice, especially to the client/patron relationship, is reflected in the nuanced and site-specific design, craftsmanship, and horticultural innovations that come alive in *Beyond Bold*. Moreover, the collaboration between patron and landscape architects has blossomed into sturdy friendships, such as those between Brady and Shelby White at the New York Botanical Garden's Native Plant Garden; and Delplace, with Cathy and Peter Halstead at Tippet Rise, a working ranch in Fishtail, Montana (where the patrons'

OPPOSITE The Garden of Contrasts, one of a collection of designed gardens at Cornerstone Sonoma in Sonoma, California, gave OvS a chance to work within an arid climate and with an alternative palette. *Agave americana* (agave) and *Allium sphaerocephalon* (drumstick allium) sparkle in the warm California sun.

vision and philanthropy have fostered a place where music, sculpture, and sustainable land stewardship coexist), and Eric Groft with Barbara Slifka, a longtime client and patron of the arts.

Slifka is a client who has worked with the firm since 1986 on some particularly complex projects. In 1998, her home overlooking the Atlantic Ocean in Sagaponack, New York, had to be moved further inland due to beach erosion. She then had the firm redesign the remaining site into a new garden, which features an abundance of giant alliums. In 2004, Groft integrated a new, smaller beach house and a pool with the garden. A close friend of both Jim and Groft, Slifka is one of the practice's most passionate ambassadors. She is also one of the patrons of the American Museum & Gardens near the historic city of Bath in the United Kingdom. The garden, which opened in 2019, can be viewed as a heartfelt homage to that long-term friendship with her, as it has some 30,000 alliums, with evocative names like 'Summer Drummer' and 'Red Mohican.' Reaching heights of up to seven feet, the plants playfully animate and accentuate the valley landscape's rolling topography. Jim was the consummate author, salesman, and proselytizing tastemaker. As we can see in *Beyond Bold*, his successors know what the OvS legacy means, and what it takes to protect and advance the art of landscape architecture as much as their brand. What was originally christened the New American Garden continues to evolve and flourish, delighting and seducing audiences.

Delplace believes that "an OvS garden is really about placemaking. [That] it's about placing people in a space that is lush and green. That the proportions work really well. [It is] where people can feel nestled or intrigued by the garden: It's almost as if you applied every adjective, and how you describe a garden, the way the light hits the leaves, the way that people walk, where you have them stop, where you have them sit." She notes that this recognition was nurtured and encouraged over time: "Jim saw to it that we would all see and experience what being in a garden at sunrise was like; what the job of physically planting bulbs in December teaches; and how to see and design for what a garden looks like in all four seasons."

According to Brady, the firm's secret lies in its "mastery of taking it from ecological to artistic." She believes that when you walk into a garden you're not focused on those individual, independent elements, such as hardscape and plant materials. Rather, the experience of the garden is an amalgam in which the hardscape is as critical as the architecture, the light, the wind, and the plants. The plants, however, do have a distinct function: "It's where our color is. It's where our texture and pattern-making is. That's key to our work." Moreover, that's the key to the three designers' shared passion.

Groft says of the firm's craft and art: "It's that balance of landscape and architecture that really makes our gardens special." Groft is passionate about Jim and Wolfgang's vital role in spotlighting horticulture. He is passionate about plants interacting equally with the man-made aspects of an OvS garden. Experiencing his gardens involves a sequence of discoveries and revelations from the opulence and abundance of the plant materials to the deliberate placement of stonework and the most discrete elements.

This book is a record of the origins, development, and full flowering of the next generation of OvS. I pen this introduction on the 30th anniversary of the September 1991 publication of *Bold Romantic Gardens: The New World Landscapes of Oehme and van Sweden*, a pioneering publication, coauthored by Susan Rademacher Frey, which advanced the art of planting design and reclaimed residential design as a hallmark of practice for leading landscape architects—thus expanding the profession's reach, influence, and scope.

In the introduction to that earlier book, landscape architect and author John O. Simonds concluded: "In our search for better cities and a more agreeable living environment we may take a clue from the innovative approaches of Oehme and van Sweden. These are engagingly described and superbly illustrated in the chapters that follow." Brady, Delplace, and Groft have adopted and adapted the theory and practice of Wolfgang Oehme and James van Sweden. As richly chronicled in *Beyond Bold*, through Inspiration, Collaboration, and Evolution, this next generation is lovingly, reverentially, and artfully advancing the OvS legacy.

CHARLES A. BIRNBAUM, FASLA, FAAR is the founder, president, and CEO of The Cultural Landscape Foundation. TCLF has had a long relationship with OvS that includes a 2009 oral history with Jim van Sweden and the 2015 travelling exhibition, *The New American Garden: The Landscape Architecture Legacy of Oehme and van Sweden*.

OPPOSITE A sculpted lawn terrace, defined by laths of Corten steel, give this Potomac, Maryland, garden a contemporary feel. Strategically placed boulders punctuate the landscape.

INSPIRATION, COLLABORATION, EVOLUTION

There's a new generation. "Bold" is now "Beyond Bold."

OvS—Oehme, van Sweden—is a firm that has been built on powerful creative vision. Initially, of course, it was the vision of the two founders, Wolfgang Oehme and James van Sweden, whose combination of superb plantsmanship and daring artistry revolutionized American landscape architecture in the 1970s and 1980s. The work of this duo, their "bold, romantic gardens," was well-chronicled at the time in magazines, newspapers, and books.

Today, however, a new generation directs the firm, and with it have come fresh achievements and different directions. New visions. Visions consonant with and derived from those of the firm's founders, but deepened, strengthened, and transformed by an evolutionary approach.

This book, *Beyond Bold*, is the story of those new achievements and new landscapes. Drawing on the legacy of the firm's founders, three current principals of the firm—Sheila Brady, Lisa Delplace, and Eric Groft—remain true to its pioneering spirit. They have synthesized the lessons they learned working with the founders. To set the stage, each of the principals will reflect on three personal and notable commissions: one that drew them to OvS, one on which they collaborated with the founding principals, and one that demonstrates how they have strengthened their foundations to build something distinctly original.

RIGHT Plantings around a 60 x 20-foot swimming pool in Southampton, New York, are set ablaze by the summer sun, and connect the nearby beach to the garden. The pool features a generous step alcove for a moment of sheltered respite.

SHEILA BRADY

"Drawing was always a way I connected with the landscape. I drew from the time I was a child and I loved it: sketching, watercolor, and pastels.

I did my undergraduate work at George Washington University because it was part of a consortium with the Corcoran Gallery of Art. It was a wonderful time; I studied everything. I took extensive drawing classes. I hadn't done painting, and I wanted to learn how to paint without drawing, but I only did a little of that. I did a lot of slab work in clay, and studied with the *National Geographic* director of photography.

My husband was an architect. He moved to MIT (Massachusetts Institute of Technology), in Cambridge, Massachusetts, for graduate studies, and I followed him up there. I thought about going into architecture, but everything turned around in one day. I was at my husband's office. By then I was very well versed in architecture, but I saw a set of plans I didn't know how to read at all. I said 'What are these? Whose are these?'

And my husband said, 'Oh those are from a really famous landscape architect, Dan Kiley.'

I had never even heard of the term landscape architect. Immediately, though, the very next day I went to the Radcliffe Institute, and found out they had a program, "An Introduction to Landscape Architecture." I enrolled in that. I loved it. I decided right then and there that I was submitting a portfolio to Harvard, to the Graduate School of Design for a Masters of Landscape Architecture.

It was a life-changing moment, seeing that set of plans in my husband John's office."

RIGHT A secluded, raised bluestone terrace in Newport, Rhode Island, overlooks the hillside toward Easton Pond. *Gaura lindheimeri* (white gaura), *Clethra alnifolia* 'Ruby Spice' (summersweet), and Rosa 'Blushing Knockout' soften the stone retaining wall.

"After graduating from Harvard, I took a job at EDAW, a leading international design firm. But I missed the immediacy I had had in the visual arts. I wanted to see gardens designed and built.

Then I saw an article about Oehme, van Sweden in *Landscape Architecture Magazine*, about the Rosenberg Garden, the 0.9-acre residential garden James and Wolfgang had created for Alex and Carole Rosenberg in Water Mill, New York. In particular, there was one image: It was an enlargement of the lavender field. I say field because it looked like it went on forever, to the water. I loved all the grasses and the blues. It reminded me of the color fields painting I had studied at the Corcoran.

I said 'That's it. That is it. I want to work in color fields in planting!'

I contacted a friend who worked at OvS, and told him how passionate I felt about the beautiful image I had seen.

I showed him some of my work. A couple of months later, I got a call from him; he said he was leaving the firm, and would I like to come in for an interview.

That was the first time I had met Wolfgang and Jim. There was immediate chemistry. Jim and I could talk about the art world. With Wolfgang, I thought he was amazing. He was very quiet, of course. But once he got to talking about plants, the plants in the plans I was showing them, that's when he got to speak up."

RIGHT An unending mackerel sky on Long Island's East End provides a dramatic backdrop to a garden adjacent to Mecox Bay in Water Mill, New York. The garden was one of the firm's first residential commissions.

"This project was a 65-acre residential landscape on a lowland coastal island in South Carolina, with a very fragile ecosystem. This project really determined how I would apply my interest in planting designs into native plantings—not strictly natives, but ensuring I was protecting the environment.

The clients were building in a planned community, Spring Island, with a strict environmental review board. Key to the community's mission was ecological development, sustainable development. It was about preserving the distinctive quality of life and the cultural heritage of the region. The island was a former rice plantation, with much of it pristine marshland. A great deal of our site, though, was an overgrown jungle. Walking through those woods, I was struck by the beauty and vigorous growth of the native saw palmettos. It was just intuitive that we were going to use native plants that were going to survive this kind of environment.

We worked with the architect for the house, William McDonough, who was known for his green architecture, and with the staff naturalist for Spring Island. We created an eight-acre native sweetgrass- and wildflower meadow on an overgrown agricultural field. I learned how to do a controlled burn, to favor the fire-adapted native vegetation, and to clear out the undergrowth beneath the beautiful saw palmettos.

We used native materials—the paths, for example, were made out of pine needles gathered from the forest itself. I had known very little about plants before I came to work at OvS, but I learned so much from Wolfgang. Particularly after this project, I was very interested in working with plants that worked with the environment."

RIGHT Live oaks, bedecked in Spanish Moss and *Muhlenbergia capillaris* (pink muhly grass) frame views over Spring Island's marshland in South Carolina. This is a quintessentially Southern vista.

"My interest in native plants as fundamental elements of a designed landscape grew with experience—notably in a 10.7-acre residential landscape we designed and installed near Denver, Colorado. The site, with its dramatic views of the Rocky Mountains, had tremendous potential.

The natural beauty had to be integrated with an imposing but minimalist house, its amenities, and the clients' desire for a more groomed environment. But as Denver receives less than 17 inches of rainfall per year, we needed to work with plants naturally adapted to such a climate. Native plants were an obvious choice, although the clients' preference for a more domesticated look called for the inclusion of adapted species as well. We were not entirely without water. There was an existing farm pond on the property which, having secured appropriate permits, we deepened and resealed, so that it could become a reservoir for irrigation, and enable adequate watering to sow an extensive meadow. Working with a local prairie seed consultant and the Denver Botanic Garden, we removed the existing cover of the site, largely a mixture of two adapted grasses, *Bromus* spp. (bromegrass) and *Agropyron cristatum* (crested wheat), and seeded in a mix of native shortgrass species such as *Bouteloua gracilis* (blue grama grass) and *Bouteloua curtipendula* (sideoats grama). A year later, the grasses were established, and we planted drifts of grassland wildflowers into them. We accommodated the requested palette of blues, whites, and purples with *Verbena stricta* (hoary vervain), *Echinacea angustifolia* (narrow-leaf coneflower) and *Dalea candida* and *D. purpurea* (white and purple prairie clover).

Tree planting became important to frame vistas and hide the human interventions in the landscape such as a pool, a tennis court, and the neighbors' house. This was done with *Abies concolor* (native white firs) and *Picea pungens* (Colorado spruces). Shelter from the intense sunlight was provided by *Populus tremuloides* (quaking aspen), *Gleditsia triacanthos var. inermis* (thornless honey locust), and *Betula populifolia* 'Whitespire Senior' (gray birch), which were chosen to harmonize with the hues of autumn in the Rocky Mountains. The integration of natural and more formal plantings was also reflected in the maintenance of the gardens. We irrigated the areas near the house, but the surrounding meadow, once established, was allowed to go dormant naturally with the seasonal summer drought, minimizing irrigation. The clients, attuned to the setting, savor the late summer through winter display of golds and russets in their personal prairie and the way it roots their property into the greater surrounding landscape."

RIGHT Denver's semi-arid climate called for native, drought-tolerant species that could abide hot, dry summers. Olson Kundig, based in Seattle, Washington, designed the house.

LISA DELPLACE

"Like Jim van Sweden, I grew up in Michigan, which has an incredibly flat, but expansive and diverse, landscape. My parents, like many in the 1950s and 1960s, had moved into a subdivision, this one outside of Detroit. It was quite beautiful, featuring grassy verges planted with majestic American elm-lined streets. But what was more interesting was that the subdivision backed up to untouched wetlands and prairie fens, and large fallow fields that had turned into meadows. That was my playground, the place where I spent most of my days. It was that seasonal, ephemeral landscape that affected me, because there was always something changing. It became part of my DNA.

Those were my early years. Later, I took up photography, sketching, and painting, and started honing my skills of observation. I began cataloging how people interfaced with the landscape. When I joined the Peace Corps, it sharpened my awareness of the cultural, social, and environmental influences on people. Later, as a landscape architect, I didn't want to replicate nature. Nature does that beautifully all on its own. I was interested in the relationship between the landscape and the people who occupy the space.

After I returned from the Peace Corps, I enrolled in the graduate program in landscape architecture at the University of Michigan. Bill Johnson (the founder of Johnson, Johnson and Roy) was teaching at the university, and I quickly became spellbound by his depth of knowledge, his keen focus on design, and his passion for the craft of landscape architecture. Along with another mentor, Bob Grese, I was interested in bringing ecological principles along with strong design sensibilities into the urban setting."

RIGHT Echoing the distant Anacostia Hills, the roof terrace at DC HQO, a collaboration with the architectural firm SmithGroup, the headquarters of DC Water, offers expansive views for impromptu meetings, open-air lunches, and is available to the public as an event space. Serving multiple functions, the garden also captures and stores storm water, an important mandate from the client. Water not absorbed is stored in cisterns and is reused throughout the property.

LISA DELPLACE **INSPIRATION**

"After graduation I wanted to focus on urban planning.
I decided to move to the East Coast to hone my skills.
I had heard quite a bit about Oehme, van Sweden, but
I wasn't familiar with their work since it was largely based
in Washington, DC.

When I went East, however, and was visiting a friend,
he happened to have an old copy of a magazine in which
Jim's house in Georgetown had been featured. As soon as
I looked at Jim's garden, I was struck, because I could see
all the landscapes of my childhood in his garden, which
was only 17 feet by 55 feet. It was amazing because he
had distilled this landscape—that was immersive, bold,
and ephemeral—into such a small space. It was all the
things I had loved as a child. It was provocative, quite
frankly, for me, because I thought, What a wonderful ability
to take the most important qualities of a meadow and be
able to apply those concepts on such a small scale.

I drove to Georgetown—at a time when Oehme, van
Sweden was located over a dress shop in Georgetown.
I had a 15-minute conversation with Jim. He said, 'Oh,
you're from Michigan; so am I. Oh, you went to the University
of Michigan; so did I. You joined the Peace Corps; I didn't,
but....' And I was hired."

RIGHT Highlighting a
new sensibility in
American landscape
design, Jim van
Sweden's bold and
innovative approach
embraced seasonal
drama and texture.

"The views of the C&O Canal, and the Potomac River, were among the main assets of the site which developer EastBanc undertook to the design of condominiums by Handel Architects along Water Street in Georgetown, Washington, DC. A power-generation substation between the planned condominium and the river was a potential obstacle. Just four-and-a-half stories high, the substation nonetheless injected a very industrial note, especially with its cement slab roof. Fortunately, the roof was designed to support the extra weight. When OvS was asked for ideas to integrate the substation into the project, Jim and I decided to turn this liability into an asset.

At the time, green roofs were still in their infancy in the United States. Pioneered in Europe, especially Germany, they were almost always covered with blankets of low-growing, succulent sedums and sod. But the construction of the substation would support soil to a greater depth than that of the standard green roof—from the usual eight inches to four feet—over the support columns. We resolved to try something more visually exciting than a sea of sedum, settling on something that had not, we thought, been done at that time: a green roof topped with prairie- or grassland plants—an elevated meadow. We knew that prairie plants had evolved to cope with drought, intense summer heat, and exposure to bitter winter winds, and believed they would flourish on this rooftop, with a rich variety of textures and colors. Knowing that the 10,000-square-foot roof would be viewed mainly from the windows of the planned condominium tower, Jim approached the planting plan like an enormous painting.

An avid art collector, he recommended we look at Helen Frankenthaler's painting *Nature Abhors a Vacuum* for inspiration. I immediately noticed how the bold swaths of yellow, blue, greens, and tan could be translated into masses of *Perovskia atriplicifolia* (Russian sage), *Rudbeckia fulgida var. sullivantii* 'Goldsturm' (Black-eyed Susan)*, and Calamagrostis* x *acutiflora* 'Karl Foerster' (feather reed grass) with punctuations of *Vitex agnus-castus* (chaste tree) and *Rosa rugosa* (shrub rose). The composition would not be accessible to the residents, but would complement the view. Since its installation in 2001, it has become a favorite of the birds who come to nest there every year, relying on the elevation of the landscape to keep them safe from predators.

As the meadow changes colors and textures throughout the seasons, it alters the view of the Potomac River beyond it in a dynamic way, bringing the naturalized riverine landscape close to the residents, and connecting them to the world around them. I have been gratified, too, to see how the plants, selected as the toughest ones Jim and I knew of, have thrived in this challenging setting."

RIGHT The elevated meadow is dramatic in every season. It is viewed as both a garden and as an abstract composition, from above.

"OvS continues to advance our knowledge in elevated gardens over structure, notably in a project I undertook at the Chicago Botanic Garden. We were involved in many aspects of refining the institution's gardens and structures. One of my foci was the design of the new Daniel F. and Ada L. Rice Plant Conservation Science Center, by the architectural firm of Booth Hansen. The five-acre project had several innovative features, including raising the building three feet above the ground so that its footprint would not diminish the site's ability to absorb storm water, a mandated function of the Botanic Garden's 500-acre campus.

To further promote the storm water absorption, we capped the building with a 16,000-square-foot demonstration-and-evaluation garden. It was an opportunity to promote the garden's plant research mission and enhance community knowledge of the benefits of green-roof technology. We divided the roof into two sections. One half was to be devoted to the evaluation of herbaceous plants—principally perennials—planted at different soil depths: eight inches, six inches, and four inches. We included some woody plants—shrubs—in the eight-inch–deep soil section. As a basis for comparison, they were planted alongside sedum strips, the best-known plants for green roofs. The other half of the roof was devoted to evaluating plants native to the Chicago area. Based on my experience at Water Street in Washington, DC, I felt confident that prairie-inspired plants would perform well, even in shallow soils. This was, in a sense, counterintuitive, because prairies typically provide deep soils. Still, my experience suggested that the prairie plant roots, once they hit the impermeable base layer of the roof, would spread horizontally.

At the Daniel F. and Ada L. Rice Plant Conservation Science Center, after a five-year trial, we proved that many of the native plants were solid performers in the prevailing green-roof conditions. In both halves, the areas open to visitors were maintained as irrigated display gardens. By contrast, the evaluation areas were irrigated only through the plants' first growing season, to allow them to become established and then subsist on natural precipitation. My takeaway was confirmation that by examining the ecological base point of plants and their origins, I could project how they would perform on the elevated landscape. When the Botanic Garden released a study of the first five years of plant performance, I was pleased that the top performers were the plants that Jim and I had selected years earlier."

RIGHT Among the many surprises on the roof of the Science Center were the plants' preferences for growth. Outriggers supporting the center's photovoltaic panels added shelter and additional moisture to the soil, beckoning some species to migrate to the perimeter.

ERIC GROFT

"One of my very early memories is of working with my grandfather in his vegetable garden. My grandmother had a couple of plots of "flaars"—that's how the Pennsylvania Dutch pronounce 'flowers.' Later, I remember walking to school from our family home in Lancaster, Pennsylvania. I grew up in a highly designed neighborhood, between the red brick market town, the carefully tended farm fields, and Piedmont Hills, dotted with covered bridges and grain silos. It wasn't quite urban, and it wasn't quite suburban. Lancaster was very distinct by having an urban core surrounded by an urban residential area, then by suburbs. Industry started popping up, and then the area transitioned to a rural agrarian landscape. I walked across a college campus to go to my more urban elementary school and my more urban junior high. I remember walking down State Street in Lancaster and I really had the sensation of understanding, from an early age, the street, the sidewalk, the setback of the houses, the rhythm of the trees—and just making myself aware of that density. Then I walked across that college campus and a city park, to a more urban setting where the houses were row houses. I recall being very conscious of that change and the transitions.

As an undergraduate interested in science, a geology class was a revelation. I related to the rocks, to the soils, and to the earth. It was something I could touch and feel. I finished a degree in geography and environmental studies. After graduation, I had an internship with a transportation planner, and I spent a summer doing survey work on covered bridges in Lancaster. I was going to some pretty remote areas, counting traffic, the number of Amish buggies, and cars. I would stop them and ask them where they were coming from and where they were going. It really made me aware of my cultural landscape. I would ask the Amish men where they were coming from. They would point and say, "Well, up the road." And I would ask where they were going to, and they would say, "Well, down the road." This began to instill in me a sense of connecting people and place.

Later, I spent two years on an environmental study of a 50,000-acre former coal field called Broad Top, a combination of deep- and surface mines. The area had been environmentally degraded and I was doing a comprehensive look at its potable water. We walked all the streams, creeks, and babbling brooks in the region—some areas that maybe hadn't been walked before or for 100 years, discovering some amazing things—groves of native hemlock trees and native trout up in the headwaters. We saw some environmental atrocities—all in all, a very sobering experience."

RIGHT Stacked stone steps, of locally quarried Deer Isle granite, descend the steep entry to a garden in Maine. Artisanal serpentine handrails follow the placement of the stone.

"A former Marine foxhole buddy of my father's during World War II, Ben Howland, a professor of landscape architecture at the University of Virginia—UVA—became a mentor and drew me to study there. When I was at UVA, Warren Byrd, my planting design instructor, took us on a field trip to Washington, DC, and our first stop was the Federal Reserve campus, a breakthrough project by OvS. Warren was talking perennial this, perennial that, sweeps of perennials, everything Oehme, van Sweden. No one had ever seen anything like it before. There were plants I had never seen. I remember being captivated by the space, a garden in the middle of Washington. I got back on the bus and asked my classmate, "So 'perennial' means it comes back every year?" The word almost didn't exist in American landscape architecture at that time."

RIGHT The New American Garden legacy began with the Virginia Avenue Gardens of the Federal Reserve, in Washington, DC, on which OvS first began work in 1977. The design of the Robert Latham Owen Fountain area, shown here prior to September 11, 2001, did not include security features, which OvS implemented in 2003.

"After I spent a couple of years working for a small
landscape architecture firm in Annapolis, Maryland, a
former classmate who worked at OvS told me that a
position was opening up there. This was back in 1986,
when Jim and Wolfgang were setting trends and everyone
in the world wanted to work for them. I was in Washington,
DC, for a meeting; I got an interview, and Jim hired me
on the spot.

Working with Jim in the early years, we would always
respond to the architecture, of course, but Jim knew when
to retire the rigidity of that and how to transition that into
nature. That is something I strive for, and that we at
OvS do best. You have to transition from Man to Nature
at some point.

A client's garden in Sagaponack, New York, was my
first project when I came onboard at OvS. It was a small
garden, a narrow lot right on the ocean. The big house on
stilts had been a little cottage but she had expanded it.

In this project, I learned all the axioms of OvS: You
wanted to celebrate all seasons, you wanted to have winter
interest, you wanted to choose plants that don't need a lot
of water or pesticides, to use plants in large masses and
large sweeps for scale. Big ocean, big sky, big sweeps for
a landscape that could read, as Jim said, driving by at 60
miles per hour. Plant a third evergreen for structure in the
garden. But no hedges. If you need a boundary, a fence, or
a wall, build it. Don't expect plants to perform architecture."

RIGHT Large granite
stepping stones lead to
a wooden gate and a
boardwalk that runs
through the house to the
ocean. The same granite
is used for the random
irregular paving for a
terrace, as well as the
oversized pool coping,
and the basking stones
around an outdoor
fireplace. Designed
within the context of
the contemporary
architecture by
Demetriades + Walker,
a firm based in Lakeville,
Connecticut, the garden
provides an intimate
seaside experience
within the vast scale
of the ocean and sky.

"Occupying nine acres along a tributary of Georgica Pond, the heart of East Hampton's most glamorous estate district, this landscape marked a major step forward for OvS, which had made its name with more modest back yards in Washington, DC. The project was also a big step forward for me. It was one of the last ones commissioned from James and Wolfgang, as they moved to a more consultatory role in the firm, I inherited the task of actually carrying out design and installation. The strength of OvS had resided in its horticultural expertise, the principals' deep knowledge of plants, and their imagination in bringing together innovative compositions drawn from natural inspirations. The project drew upon other skills, however. The clients, a couple with two children, were somewhat atypical of the Hamptons. They didn't favor the broad swaths of golf course–worthy turf that characterizes so many of the estates in that region. Rather, they preferred to embrace the natural beauties of the site, clearing less than two acres, and leaving the rest to its native cover of mature oak woods.

The clients reacted very positively to my suggestions that we strive to integrate the house with its setting. Taking a cue from the vegetation that bordered Georgica Pond, we used plantings of the indigenous species—*Panicum virgatum* (switchgrass) and *Rudbeckia maxima* (large coneflower), for instance—to draw the views of the water up to and even through the house. Designed in a soaring contemporary style by the Bridgehampton, New York-based firm of Barnes Coy Architects, the structure has a central glass-walled living room that brings the view of the creek right into the heart of the residence. The landscape also seems to run through the house, under a wooden walkway that functions as a low bridge, and into an interior courtyard.

We also persuaded the clients to move the parking area away from the very front of the house, so that the front door could be approached on foot, lending the residence the feeling of being immersed in the landscape. Also, we moved the swimming pool a distance down the slope from the house, raising it up so that instead of enclosing it, as building codes demanded with an obtrusive fence, we substituted a four-foot-high retaining wall, which does not interrupt the view. A small but telling detail is how we built seating and other furniture into the architecture that defined the outdoor spaces. The project marked a departure for OvS, as it contributed to a change in the firm's reputation. While we had been seen as masters of planting, under the new generation, we now became known for our mastery of hardscape, as well."

RIGHT The long pool and spa are surrounded by a profusion of grasses and summer-blooming perennials. An overpass connects the pool terrace to an outdoor living room with a fireplace and a dining terrace fragrant with herbs.

2

HOUSE AND ITS GARDEN

At OvS, our roots—literally as well as metaphorically—are in residential design. The genesis of the firm lay in the garden that James van Sweden and Wolfgang Oehme designed for the back yard of Jim's house in the Georgetown neighborhood of Washington, DC. They transformed Jim's modest, 17-foot by 55-foot space into something revolutionary in the American landscape architecture of that time: A garden that despite its diminutive size succeeded in being dramatic, lush, and beautiful in all seasons, and both by night as well as by day.

This garden would inspire all the young landscape architects who subsequently joined OvS. More immediately, it inspired a clientele, initially neighbors in Georgetown who wanted OvS to transform their residential spaces. The fledgling firm expanded its activities up and down the East Coast, across the nation, and overseas. The scope of OvS came to include all sorts of landscapes, public and commercial, as well as private. Yet we have never lost our enthusiasm for residential design.

The process of that design has changed. With the introduction of a younger generation, it ceased to be a back-of-the-napkin affair and began to include meticulous and detailed plans. But the intrinsic and essential balance achieved by the firm's founders remains at its core and horticulture, a love for and a knowledge of plants, was returned to American landscape design, married with a profound mastery of architecture. So, the experience of one of our residential gardens typically begins with being overwhelmed by colors, textures, fragrances, and the structure and movement of the plants. Gradually, this is joined by a recognition of the bones: the paving, the walls, the fences, the sequencing of garden rooms, and attention to the architectural detail.

A central characteristic of our residential design is a deep dive into making the landscape site-specific. We like to be a part of a conversation about a project before the architecture is fully conceived, so that we can maximize how the house is positioned on the site. We focus intensively on understanding the intrinsic characteristics of the site, and how the composition and harmony, and sometimes the juxtaposition, of the site, garden, and house will work.

A large part of our preparation is the creation of a cultural landscape inventory. This includes an in-depth look at geography, topography, ecology, soils, and the history of the site. The inventory reveals the indigenous characteristics that make the site unique, and so will inform the design.

The process is also client-centric. Homes, after all, are quintessentially personal. In each project, we engage deeply with our clients to make sure that the design program reflects their desires and their aspirations. We want the landscape to reflect not only what they want now, but also what they seem likely to want in the future. What does the horizon look like in five or 10 years, and will that change design decisions?

Another aspect of our residential design is that we like to cluster related elements together so that the landscape becomes a tableau of how the clients live their lives and how they engage with the outdoors. Ultimately, the process is about mapping out the journey from the front entry through the house and through the various gardens.

Once, the architect, Ira Grandberg, who had recommended us to a residential client, was asked what makes OvS special. He cited how thoroughly we explore the history and cultural aspects of each property and how we base design decisions on that. Grandberg explained that our practice is to present several design alternatives that reflect the clients' desires and needs, and then let them choose the elements from each that they like, to create a composite. He also mentioned our white-glove service that puts the gardens into the ground. As our founders believed, and what still holds true today: "We are not afraid to roll up our sleeves and get dirty" to create a great garden.

OPPOSITE Limestone steps descend from the house to a Mediterranean-inspired White Garden on a hillside in McLean, Virginia. *Achillea millefolium* 'New Vintage White' (yarrow), *Anemone x hybrida* 'Honorine Jobert' (windflower) and *Baptisia alba* (white wild indigo) comprise a part of the white-flowering species in the garden.

RIGHT The garden of a 19th-century farmhouse on the Rappahannock River in Virginia, features a profusion of native American meadow plantings. The house was exquisitely renovated by the architectural firm, Neumann Lewis Buchanan, based in Washington, DC.

RIGHT A granite millstone fountain masquerades among a sea of plantings at a townhouse garden in Washington, DC's Georgetown.

OPPOSITE TOP This residential garden, once a concrete pad that led to a garage, is now a richly textured series of spaces. A rectilinear pool set on the bias is a perfect setting for a favorite sculpture.

OPPOSITE BOTTOM Widely recognized as OvS' first residential commission, the structure of this 50-year-old garden just outside Baltimore, Maryland, has remained largely unchanged since its installation. It has, however, matured into a verdant sanctuary.

RIGHT A rose garden on Lily Pond Lane in East Hampton, New York, is even more seductive in the late afternoon sun. *Rosa* 'Rosarium Uetersen,' *Rosa* 'Jolie Vernada,' and *Rosa* 'Penelope' make up a part of the myriad roses in the garden. OvS collaborated with the New York-based John B. Murray Architect, and the New York interior design firm of Cullman & Kravis on the Harrie T. Lindeberg-designed home.

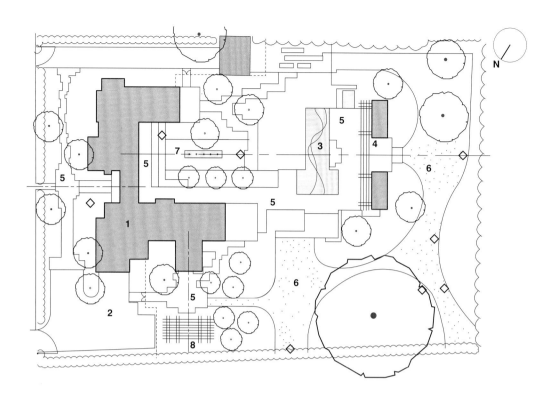

SITE PLAN
1. Residence
2. Forecourt
3. Pool
4. Arbor
5. Terrace
6. Lawn
7. Water Feature
8. Dining Pavilion

OPPOSITE White-blooming plants—*Rosa* 'Seafoam' roses and *Lysimachia clethroides* (gooseneck loosestrife)—light up the entry garden's four-season planting of textural evergreens. *Aster mongolicus* (Mongolian aster) is just coming into bloom, *lower left*.

The cultural landscape inventory played a particularly influential role in informing the design of this project.

The project was especially significant because of its location in Amagansett, New York, a town that lies at the eastern end of the Hamptons, the storied string of resorts on the South Fork of Long Island. New construction has threatened to change the character of this area, but in partnership with the client and the design team—specifically the Amagansett, New York-based James D'Auria Architect and Fury Design, an interior design firm in Philadelphia, Pennsylvania—we were determined to make this landscape a celebration of the neighborhood's distinctive geographical character, halfway between the Atlantic Ocean and the famed potato fields of Long Island.

The site was assembled by joining two adjacent lots to create a just-over-an-acre property. The rambling farmhouse adopted the architectural vernacular of the district with a grey, shingled exterior and a low, peaked roof. Privacy—and integration with its surroundings—was ensured by a privet hedge, iconic in the Hamptons, and which surrounds the entire property. Two wings of the house enclose a compact area to its rear, forming a courtyard. We graded this area to a depth of three steps to create a sunken garden. This added a bit of topography to what is otherwise a rather flat site, and also increased the sense of enclosure. To enhance the farmhouse aspect, we made the central feature of this area a long rectangular trough such as a farmer of the past might have maintained to water the livestock.

The clients were not enamored with turf, although they did want us to include a compact recreational lawn toward the rear of the property. For the rest, they preferred a lush tapestry of perennial plantings. These began in a bed flanking the sunken courtyard and continued through a series of ornamental meadows embracing the swimming pool and its twin pavilions. The overall effect is soft, luxuriant, and romantic—a celebration of the seasons. This planting also created a sense of intimacy in the T-shaped swimming pool, which we took advantage of by placing submerged seating benches to encourage conversation among the swimmers.

Special experiences were inserted into the landscape. An outdoor dining pavilion adjacent to the house was furnished with a window cut into the perimeter hedge, to provide a view of a picturesque old cemetery. One of the two lots that had been joined to create this landscape had been a small working nursery. A spectacular, 100-year-old specimen beech was preserved and the area under its pendulous branches was planted with *Carex pensylvanica* (woodland sedge) to create a foliage-enclosed secret garden. Along the southern border of the landscape, at the end of the service drive, we installed a compact kitchen garden, whose raised bed was enclosed in Corten steel.

One of the most pleasant challenges of the commission was collaborating with the clients and design team on the installation of a collection of outdoor sculpture. These included six large and assertive pieces, each of which demanded its own distinctive setting. Placement hinged on finding or creating the correct spots to complement the artworks by such international sculptors as Bernar Venet, Jun Kaneko, Ugo Rondinone, Mark Manders, Joel Shapiro, and Mark di Suvero.

RIGHT Twin pavilions connected by an arbor mark the western boundary of the swimming pool, with a lounge on the left, and a bar and kitchen on the right. A living, blooming balustrade of *Nepeta* x *faassenii* 'Walker's Low' (catmint) and *Perovskia atriplicifolia* (Russian sage) punctuates the limestone terrace.

OVERLEAF LEFT *Untitled, Left and Right*, by Japanese ceramic artist Jun Kaneko is silhouetted against a backdrop of *Thuja standishii* x *plicata* 'Green Giant' (arborvitae) and framed by *Helianthus salicifolius* (willow-leaved sunflower), *left*, and *Amsonia hubrichtii* (bluestar), *right*.

OVERLEAF RIGHT A monumental head by the Dutch artist Mark Manders nestles into a sea of *Petasites japonicus* (butterbur).

RIGHT Three stone totems by the New York-based Swiss artist Ugo Rondinone march down the path into a wooded corner.

RIGHT The view from the kitchen looks out through a cinnamon-barked copse of *Lagerstroemia indica x fauriei* (crepe myrtle) to a piece by the American sculptor Mark di Suvero that echoes the trees' criss-crossing trunks.

RIGHT A dramatic Long Island sky was captured on the surface of the swimming pool, whose interior was deliberately coated with a dark finish to enhance the reflectivity of the water.

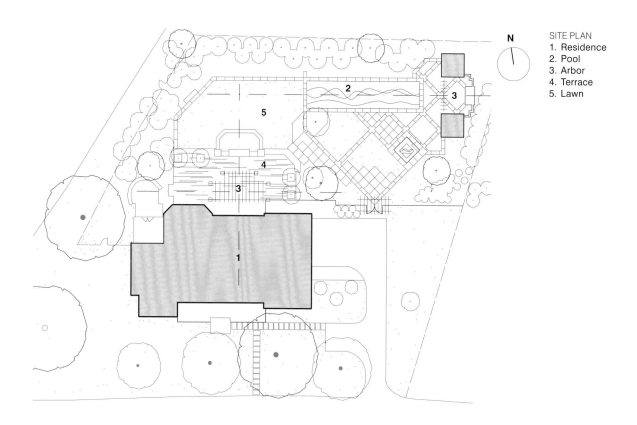

SITE PLAN
1. Residence
2. Pool
3. Arbor
4. Terrace
5. Lawn

OPPOSITE Arching jets
of water crisscross
the pool, bringing to
life a view of the fireplace
and pool pavilion, which
was designed by Boggs
Partners Architects
in Annapolis, Maryland.

It might seem that a 'smaller landscape' requires less work
to design, but in fact it can take considerable ingenuity to
fit all the necessary pieces together in a tight space. The
quarter of an acre behind the house—somewhat small for
a suburban garden but a bit larger than most urban yards—
required a fresh and imaginative approach, especially since
the clients had a large wish list that included a swimming
pool, a spa, and an outdoor fireplace and kitchen to be
added to an existing arbor. Compounding the challenge
of fitting all of these pieces together were the stringent
environmental regulations of the Chesapeake Bay area.
There was a strict limit on the number of impervious
surfaces that could be included, and the need to avoid
disturbing an existing septic field.

An obvious solution would be to connect the house
and swimming pool with a paved surface, but this was
impossible because of the interposition of the septic field.
Instead, we attached a deck to the back of the house,
spacing the decking boards far enough apart so that any
precipitation could drain through to the earth below and so
ensure that it would qualify as a pervious surface. To avoid
any disturbance to the septic system, we rested the deck
on steel beams cantilevered out from the house. Drywells,
strategically placed throughout the property, manage
rainfall and mitigate much of the surface runoff.

The location of the landscape atop a bluff overlooking

the Severn River provided a commanding view of the city
of Annapolis to the west, which was unfortunately not
visible from the back of the house, which faces north. So
we created a view for the family room and kitchen by
installing a large, raised planter at the north side of the
deck. A massive granite bench set along the side of the
deck absorbs solar radiation on sunny days, furnishing a
cozy spot to enjoy an early spring or late fall day.

Another effect of the limitation on impervious surfaces
within the garden was to restrict the terrace at the head of
the pool to a compact area. We avoided a rectilinear
treatment that could be boring by rotating the pattern of the
pavement 45 degrees, which seems to expand the space and
creates a more dynamic-feeling experience.

Integrating the swimming pool into the garden was
another challenge, but also essential because it was such a
significant feature of this relatively small space. We backed
it up against a pair of ornamental pavilions, between which
we set the outdoor fireplace. Another feature was inspired
by a trip that the principal-in-charge of the team had recently
made to Spain, with a visit to the Alhambra, in Granada.
A famous aspect of this complex is the Courtyard of the
Canal, in which jets of water arch out from either side of a
linear pool. We borrowed this detail but simplified it,
transforming the swimming pool into a fully functioning
decorative element of the garden space.

RIGHT An existing arbor was reclad and painted a dark green to provide an elegant frame for the view from the family room and kitchen area of the residence.

RIGHT Inspired by a visit to the Alhambra in Granada, Spain, these jets add an aural and visual element, and the movement of water to the garden.

RIGHT The enticing glow
in the garden invites
evening relaxation with
family and friends or a late
night swim. The pavilions
are designed by Boggs
Partners Architects,
in Annapoilis, Maryland.

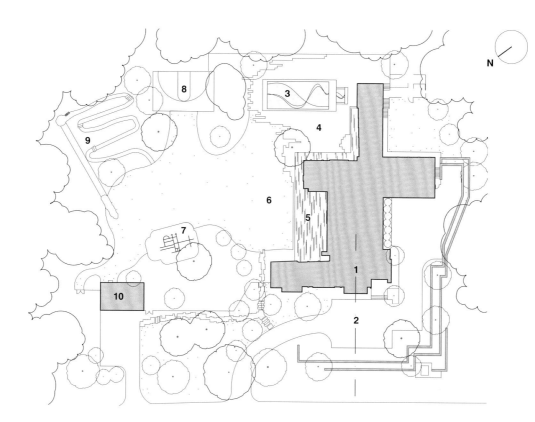

SITE PLAN
1. Residence
2. Forecourt
3. Pool
4. Terrace
5. Deck
6. Lawn
7. Play Space
8. Sports Court
9. Sledding Hill
10. Guest House

N

OPPOSITE The emphatic
verticals of the
Phyllostachys aurea
(golden bamboo)
echoes and reinforces
the lines of the
architecture's geometric
planes in the entryway
garden, seamlessly
linking the interior
and exterior spaces.

The landscape for a new home for a large, tight-knit family
needed to accommodate not only the family's six children
but also to serve as an entertainment center and gathering
place for their friends and other members of the extended
family. While the two-acre site seemed ample for a suburban
property, it was a challenge to fit in all the features the clients
desired—a swimming pool and spa, a multiuse sports court,
a pergola, a guesthouse, a tree house, a kitchen garden,
and a lawn large enough for impromptu soccer games—as
well as space for the lush perennial border whose prospect
had originally attracted the clients to OvS.

We collaborated closely with the architect, Alan
Dynerman, of the Washington, DC-based firm Dynerman
Architects, as well as with the clients, to provide the natural
beauty through the seasons that the clients desired—while
organizing the landscape in a logical fashion. How would the
children go from the play areas to the pool and the vegetable
garden, and then perhaps back to the pool? These issues
had to be carefully considered to make sure they worked.

We optimized the topography of the site so that each
feature had its own space yet was part of the greater
composition. Taking cues from the contemporary style of
the house we extended the geometry into the site, providing
an opportune way to allow the landscape and architecture
to mesh as one. In addition to their desire for all of these
functional elements, the clients were also keenly focused
on aesthetics. The various amenities were concealed either
by topography or by broad sweeps of plants so that,
as the clients desired, the view from the residence was of
an abundant garden.

One of our strengths is the commitment to stay
engaged with clients. We return every spring to help the
children plant the vegetable garden; we help with sowing
the seeds and setting out seedlings; and we develop
calendars for harvesting. This has enriched our experience,
and the clients' too, as we pursue an ongoing relationship
over greening the landscape and digging deeper into
nature in their back yard.

RIGHT A back view of the house and yard illustrates the use of plantings to create garden "rooms" and coordinates with the activity areas of the house. A sweep of lawn continues the open plan of the kitchen and family room. The pool area is more intimate, taking its cue from an indoor–outdoor covered porch. Dividing the two spaces is a *Cercidiphyllum japonicum* (katsura tree), installed as a mature specimen to make a statement that is in scale with the house.

OVERLEAF LEFT Nestled into a semi-enclosed court at the back of the house, the veranda provides an outdoor living space with a view of the mature woodland beyond.

OVERLEAF RIGHT The clients' desire for bold flowers resulted in almost four seasons of bloom, from early spring bulbs to the last fall asters. In this garden detail, a mass of *Hydrangea paniculata* 'Tardiva' (panicle hydrangea) serves not only as screening but also as a source of summer-long blooms, and a mounded contrast to the upright inflorescence flowers of the *Pennisetum alopecuroides* (fountain grass) in front.

RIGHT Rectangular garden beds inset into the margins of the pool terrace help to modulate the space and fit it into the niche created by the architecture. Serving the needs of the clients' very active children dictated that this area be distinct from the more laid-back aesthetic of the rest of the landscape.

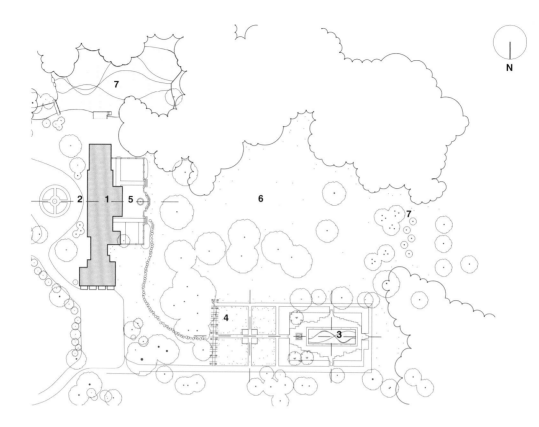

SITE PLAN
1. Residence
2. Forecourt
3. Pool
4. Arbor
5. Terrace
6. Lawn
7. Pond

The chance to revitalize a neglected work by a revered 20th century landscape architect was to be approached in between elements that honor the past and also serve the present generation. For years, the clients discussed buying a second house where the entire family could be together for holidays and could enjoy as a weekend getaway. Knowing how busy their lives were, however, we accepted that their dream might well remain just that. We were thrilled when the father phoned us to say he had found a great house in nearby Lake Forest, Illinois.

Called Thorndale Manor, the house came with a landscape by Jens Jensen, a Danish immigrant who, after joining the Chicago Parks Department, fell in love with the regional flora and became a key figure in creating the Prairie Style of landscape design, often collaborating with the architect Howard Van Doren Shaw. Our immediate advice to the family was, "Buy." Three hours later, the clients called back to say that they had submitted an offer.

Completed in 1916, the house was originally set on 20 acres, but now included a landscape of about seven-and-a-half acres. The manor house retained its majestic presence, and the landscaping held many significant remnants. Our challenge was to create a setting for the house that would satisfy the needs of a modern extended family, while also respecting Jensen's original ideas—and restoring them where we could.

We contacted the University of Michigan, which maintains one of the principal archives of Jensen's papers, and were able to locate original drawings of the Thorndale landscape. Future work will involve the expansion of the perennial borders as detailed in Jensen's papers and his signature "dog-leg meadow," which extends the landscape just around a bend or out of view, thus obscuring its end and suggesting that such meadows were longer than they were.

During the 2020 COVID-19 pandemic, the family retreated to the manor and began a period of intense exploration of the house's surroundings, a treasure hunt with Jensen's plans serving as the treasure maps. They traced old paths and the outlines of former parterres, even locating the foundation of a former chicken coop and a small livestock barn. There has been encouragement, too, in the enthusiasm shown by all the generations of the family about restoring this landscape and residence. Not just inhabitants, they have become stewards of the work of Jensen and Van Doren Shaw.

RIGHT The roundel that a circular driveway creates in front of the house is also part of the original design, though it has been replanted several times in the century since its installation. In its present incarnation, the roundel is a parterre garden of *Buxus sempervirens* (common box) whose interior spaces are planted each spring with annuals.

RIGHT Howard Van Doren Shaw designed many of the houses in this community, and often included a formal terrace attached to the residence. We restored the fountain, finding a new centerpiece to fit inside its basin and return it to life.

RIGHT The swimming
pool, high on the clients'
wish list, is a new feature
of the landscape, and was
integrated into a division
of what had originally
been an extensive kitchen
and cutting garden.
The surrounding *Fagus
sylvatica* (European
beech) hedge, when
established, will obscure
this intervention.

RIGHT A drone photograph shows the layout of the seven-and-a-half acres remaining from the original 20 acres of the property. The "dogleg meadow," a characteristic feature of Jensen's designs, ends by disappearing behind a screen of trees to fool the eye and suggest a greater expanse.

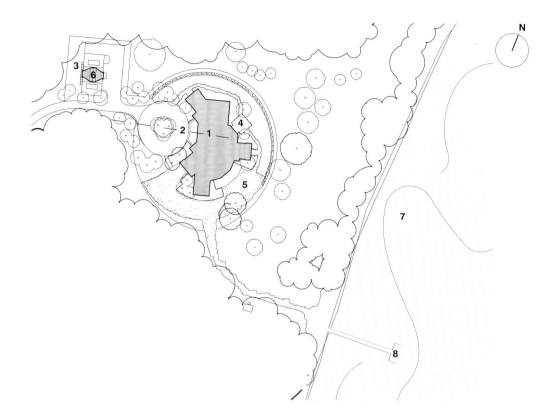

SITE PLAN
1. Residence
2. Forecourt
3. Arbor
4. Terrace
5. Lawn
6. Vegetable Garden
7. Atlantic Ocean
8. Dock

Set on a low outwash moraine close to a salt pond, the 20-acre tract of island real estate offers a choice example of an exceedingly rare habitat, sand plain grassland. The environmentally sensitive owners were determined to preserve its biological integrity while making it their family home. To do this, the house and horse barn were carefully located in the landscape, constructed with minimal disturbance, and arranged so as to complement the natural features.

The house was inset into a 150-foot-diameter circular space at the northeastern edge of the area. Inside this restricted space, the landscape was domesticated with plantings of both native and adapted plants common on the island: Compact trees such as *Amelanchier canadensis* (serviceberry) and shrubs such as *Aronia arbutifolia* (chokeberry) and *Buddleia* 'Black Knight' (butterfly bush), *Ilex* spp. (holly), native *Morella pensylvanica* (bayberry) and *Rosa* 'Knockout.' The lawn was limited to a narrow crescent. Outside of the low, encircling retaining wall and stone path, the native vegetation was left undisturbed, to the extent possible, and where that was unavoidable, the fabric of plants was replanted with appropriate natives grown from seed collected locally so that the new vegetation would be authentic not only in species, but even in its regionally adapted types.

As with cutting and polishing a gem, landscape features were included in such a way as to heighten the experience of place. So, the entrance drive was woven through the native pitch pine woods, then brought out along the edge of an existing meadow to expose the visitor to the beautiful sea island light and the expansiveness of the native grassland, before swinging back into the woods to complete the trip to the house. The barn, paddock, and attendant vegetable and cutting gardens were also set at the meadow's edge, to take advantage of the views. The guesthouse, hidden in the woods, was connected to the main house by one of the riding and walking paths that have been threaded through the property.

The approach to the house was deliberately simple and unpretentious, without the usual auto court so often seen, and was lined with natives: *Vaccinium* (blueberry), and meadow plants, such as *Sporobolus heterolepis* (prairie dropseed), *Asclepias tuberosa* (orange butterfly weed), and *Liatris spicata* (blazing star). A circular drive allows cars to pull up in front of the house, but they are then diverted to a garage set discretely back at the edge of an adjacent meadow, so that the overall impression is one of emerging from the natural landscape. The lines between the designed and natural gardens intertwine throughout the property and blur the lines between people and nature.

RIGHT Perennials and native grasses hide the wall that edges the interior domesticated zone, blurring the transition and enabling an uninterrupted view into the native scene beyond, helping to integrate the two landscapes into a single whole.

OVERLEAF LEFT The view across the garden to the house, which was designed by Roger Ferris + Partners of Westport, Connecticut, includes a stone birdbath wreathed in *Verbena bonariensis* (purpletop vervain) and, beyond, *Perovskia atriplicifolia* (Russian sage). Such plants were introduced into the garden zone to enrich its color palette and extend the bloom throughout the growing season.

OVERLEAF RIGHT The garden's bluestone terrace, set with handmade furniture from Munder Skiles, overlooks Katama Bay and the Atlantic Ocean.

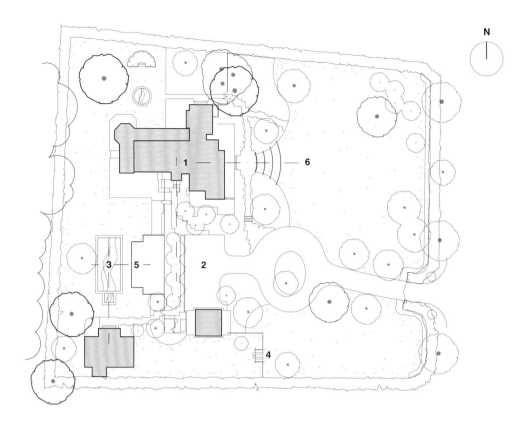

SITE PLAN
1. Residence
2. Forecourt
3. Pool
4. Arbor
5. Terrace
6. Lawn

A classic of Hamptons Shingle Style architecture, this turn-of-the-20th-century mansion is located just a few blocks from the ocean and occupies one of the most imposing estates in the town of Southampton, the storied beach resort on Long Island's South Fork. We were called in by the project architect, John B. Murray, to be part of the team to update the residence and grounds. The New York-based designer Victoria Hagan created the interiors.

While Murray was reorganizing the interior of the house and renovating the carriage house as a guest cottage, we set to work on the two-acre landscape. Aside from a couple of fine old trees, including a massive *Quercus cerris* (Turkey oak), there was little of note on the grounds besides a too-small, poorly placed swimming pool that was out of scale with the house and jammed between the residence and the northwest corner of the property. The update began with the decision to move and expand the pool.

Working within the landscape vernacular of the community, we selected a local classic, hydrangeas, to serve as the backbone of the plantings around the house. Rather than lining them up in the typical row along the front of the house, we planted a generous swath of 200 shrubs in large drifts of varying types: *Hydrangea macrophylla* 'Kardinal' (bigleaf hydrangea) to the north of the house, *Hydrangea serrata* 'Blue Billow' (mountain hydrangea) along its front, and drifts of *Hydrangea macrophylla* 'All-Summer Beauty' (bigleaf hydrangea) flanking the

broad, curved lawn steps that serve as the grand approach to the house's front entrance.

For the convenience of the residents, we also installed a substantial and inviting path from the parking area abutting the south wall of the house and the front entrance. For this we used another local standby, bluestone pavers, placed in a random pattern at four-inch intervals so that the stone appeared inset into the turf of the lawn to create a tapestry-like effect.

The swimming pool was relocated to the rear of the house and expanded to a more appropriate 60- by 20-foot size. This was enveloped in a sea of pink flowers—pink being the favorite color of the client's. A pool house alongside the pool served two design functions: It separates the pool from an adjacent parking-service area, and turns the site of the pool into a landscape destination.

The owners of the house wanted modern conveniences but a "legacy" look, so we enhanced the lawn with mature trees of appropriate types. *Aesculus hippocastanum* (horse chestnut) is another local fixture, and we included a magnificent specimen found at a local nursery. On a neighborhood garden tour, we had admired the *Tilia americana* (American linden) trees at another estate, the broad boughs sweeping down almost to the ground, and we also planted a specimen of that. In June, the linden's white flowers fill the yard with a sweet fragrance, adding to the sensuality of the planting.

RIGHT Carefully massed shrubs such as *Buxus sempervirens* (common box) contribute to the architecture that defines a series of garden rooms around the house. *Geranium* 'Rozanne' (hardy geranium) furnishes color from late spring into mid-fall.

RIGHT Bold planting was essential to marrying the classic Hamptons mansion to its new setting.

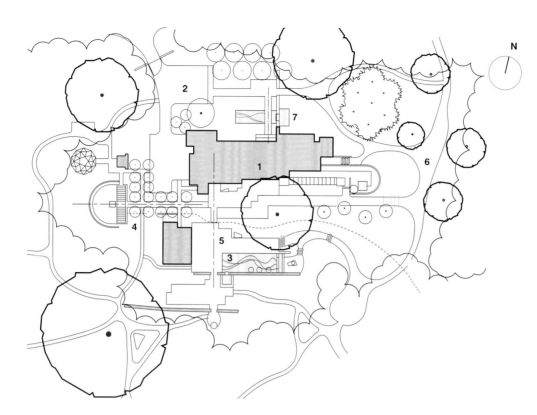

SITE PLAN
1. Residence
2. Forecourt
3. Pool
4. Arbor
5. Terrace
6. Lawn
7. Pond

N

Located on five acres of former pastureland in the more rural backcountry of Greenwich, Connecticut, the project began with the removal and replacement of an existing house with one more suitable for the clients' large family and special interests. We were involved from the early stages of the project—a collaboration with Carol Kurth Architecture, of Bedford, New York, and Laura Bohn Design Associates, New York, New York. The site was set on a glacial ridge overlooking a clearing and a wooded slope. In a nod to the property's past and to the topography, the house was aligned with the rustic stone walls that marked the edges of erstwhile paddocks. The development of the landscape took its cue from these two factors.

The couple who built the house had met through their mutual love of the tango and their predilection for drama. But it is drama within a disciplined context, which marked both the house and the landscape. For example, disciplined drama describes the house's front entrance, where a path crosses a two-level water feature on a bridge of stepping-stones made of finely finished bluestone slabs. More stones continue in a progression to an arrival court, to supply a generous and elegant approach.

The planting in front of the house is also controlled, principally in hues of green, and focused on texture and form. This foliar tapestry is accented by whites, as white birches were a favorite of the wife's Russian roots. The color of the chalky bark was picked up by successive waves of seasonal blooms—white crocus in early spring, followed by white daffodils, and white wood asters in the fall.

Behind the house, rectangular, interlocked terraces ascend the slope in a stately dance, providing space for a

spa, an allée of fruit trees, and a vegetable garden with a chicken coop. The placement of the swimming pool was dictated by topography and geology, with one end elevated above grade. A vanishing edge allows the water to spill out over that end of the pool and down a glass wall, to create shimmering refractions. A fire bowl sits on a block of local granite to ensure the display continues into the night. Upslope from the pool is a retaining wall of Roxbury granite quarried in Connecticut, which functions as the backstop of a fountain. The spouts that recirculate water into the pool were inspired by a detail from a garden in Toledo, Spain.

The planting at the back of the house is, in contrast with that of the front, lush and romantic, more typical of the masses of perennials for which OvS is renowned. The pool enclosure required by local code is supplied by a row of narrow steel pickets, whose slender, upright form is echoed by the stems of the grasses. Bluestone shards are used again here to pave an open-air dance floor. The bluestone theme was set aside in the vicinity of the pool because that dark stone collects solar radiation and on sunny days it can heat up to become uncomfortably hot underfoot. Here, a pavement of natural cleft Roxbury granite was used, which was woven into the bluestone floor of the pool house.

Every effort was made to honor the wooded character of the site. Trees were preserved where possible during the construction and moved when necessary. The developed landscape was integrated into the surrounding woodland with meandering paths designed to provide pleasant, shady strolls. In the winter, when the leaves have fallen, the views roll off almost all the way to Long Island Sound.

RIGHT View of the entryway from the auto court. New York bluestone pavers give way to Roxbury granite paving. A rough block of Roxbury granite is set up on blocks over the bluestone to serve as a bench; at night, a light hidden underneath the granite block enhances the illusion that the stone is floating.

RIGHT The entry garden viewed from above. Bluestone walks are interwoven with a terrace of paler Roxbury granite; the insistent linearity of the granite slabs is relieved with the insertion of intermittent diagonal crevices. Block plantings of yellow–green *Pieris japonica* (Japanese andromeda) echo the form of the house and reflecting pool.

OVERLEAF LEFT Flanking the front door are oversized pots by Atelier Vierkant, planted with bold-leaved tropicals, including *Alocasia macrorrhiza* (elephant ears).

OVERLEAF RIGHT A grove of *Betula papyrifera* (paper birch) in front of the house provides a nostalgic detail for the Russian-descended homeowner. The mirror-polished, stainless steel sculpture by David Harber captures and redisplays the surrounding landscape.

RIGHT Greenery—
Hakonechloa macra
(Japanese forest grass)
on the left and *Carex
morrowii* 'Ice Dance'
(Japanese sedge) on the
right—embraces and
softens the edges of the
hardscape, which
includes a plant container
by Kornegay Design.

108

RIGHT The swimming pool's water-return spouts were inspired by a detail observed in a garden in Toledo, Spain.

RIGHT No space is wasted in this garden: A nook below the swimming pool is transformed into an irresistible retreat with the addition of a fire feature set on a huge block of granite and by the replacement of the end of the swimming pool with a glass wall over which the water cascades in sheets into a plunge pool.

RIGHT The geometry of the Secret Garden is apparent from above. The garden is entered through a door from the master bedroom. The spa (at center) is surrounded by *Magnolia virginiana* (sweetbay magnolia) and *Stewartia koreana* (Korean stewartia), which provide privacy and late-spring to mid-summer bloom.

GATHERING PLACES

Designing a landscape for people to gather in shares many characteristics with other branches of design and yet is distinctly different. Common to both is the emphasis on assessing and developing the potential of the site, on consulting the needs and desires of the clients, and on working with the local ecology and cultural context.

Yet there are unique features about designing public spaces. In a place where people gather, one must satisfy an array of clients and stakeholders from parks departments or foundations, to the corporate or museum board that is commissioning the work, to who will or will not be the primary users.

Sometimes, as on a university campus, it is relatively easy to profile the users that will consist of students, faculty, and parents. In other scenarios, as in a public garden or arboretum, or a museum, the user base is a broader, more demographically diverse public united by a common interest. The diversities of the visitors mean that creating a single program for gathering involves the orchestration of several parts. As designers, we must understand how people move and behave in groups, while still accommodating the solitary individual. Landscape must be legible and functional for both the many and the few.

Such complex landscape programs demand a special focus on and insight into how people will use the space, and adapting the space to that usage. Sculpting the land and designing its circulation is quite different in a solemn public memorial than in a shopping space, yet both depend on an understanding of human nature and how people function in public places. These spaces must be at once flexible and programmable, active, and compelling.

OvS brings a unique sensibility to the design of public-gathering spaces: A horticultural richness, with all of its tactile, visual, and sensory experiences. Far from a static backdrop, these landscapes add biodiversity to the local ecology and are filled with movement, fragrance, and subtle harmonies of color. As the following pages will make clear, we continued to redefine the place of assembly as exciting and gratifying as any private garden, but also uniquely itself with every iteration.

OPPOSITE Since 1986, OvS has collaborated with the firms of New York-based Peter Marino Architect and the Manhasset, New York, company Castagna Realty at Americana Manhasset, a luxury shopping destination in Manhasset, New York. Perennial plantings and seasonal rotations reflect the haute couture shown in the stores, and reinforce the opulence of the brands, the architecture, and the sculpture.

RIGHT The United States Embassy in Bridgetown, Barbados, was converted from an existing but unfinished office building located on a former coral quarry. The project's architect was the Washington, DC, firm SORG Architects, with whom we have enjoyed many collaborations. Security is a primary concern for any federal building, and the approach began by encircling the site with ornamental fencing. We were required to provide separate entrances for each category of visitor to the embassy, including a "grand entrance" proportioned to accommodate distinguished guests arriving by limousine. The approach winds up the hill to an elegant court and garden ornamented with *Roystonea regia* (royal palm), special paving, and a cooling water feature that was very welcome in the hot and seasonally humid Barbados climate. Other entrances provide access for the staff, visitors seeking to secure passports or visas, and a vehicular access for truck deliveries. Each entrance required separate gates and a carefully orchestrated network of paths and drives. The planting emphasized robust ground covers, such as *Helianthus debilis* (beach sunflower), *Wedelia trilobata* (wedelia), *Ruellia brittoniana* (Mexican petunia), and *Tradescantia spathacea* (boat lily), that require minimal upkeep, with some ironclad, adapted bulbs such as *Clivia miniata* (bush lilies) and *Crinum asiaticum* (giant crinum lilies) for color. Unlike other embassy landscapes that we have designed, in which the grounds had to be kept clear of any planting that might shelter intruders, in Barbados we were allowed to plant trees. In fact, their shade is virtually a necessity in the brilliant tropical sunshine. Accordingly, we sheltered the grounds with *Swietenia mahagoni* (Mahogany), *Azadirachta indica* (Indian lilac neem tree), and palms.

RIGHT The German-American Friendship Garden is located on the National Mall in Washington, DC, between the White House and the Washington Monument. The garden celebrates the German-American Tricentennial, the third anniversary of the German settlement in America. OvS designed the original garden in 1983, which was dedicated by President Ronald Reagan in 1988. In 2013, the firm updated the garden with 2,500 new perennials, shrubs, grasses, and ground cover.

When we first visited the American Museum & Gardens in its rural setting outside Bath, England, in the summer of 2012, we had a remarkable experience. The museum's galleries, housed in an 1820 Georgian manor house, showcase artifacts and period rooms through a rich and unbroken history of the American decorative arts, from the early colonial period to the eve of the American Civil War and beyond.

The exhibits extended to the outdoors, but just barely. Within the 125 acres of grounds, we found a replica of George Washington's Mount Vernon garden that was in need of renovation, a somewhat haphazard and neglected arboretum of American trees, and the rudiments of a Lewis and Clark National Historical Trail. Unlike the carefully conceived indoor displays, the outdoor spaces were disconnected, with poorly designed pedestrian paths. We were asked for a proposal for a truly American landscape, but soon realized that the project would have to begin with a comprehensive reorganization.

A new master plan defined the grounds as a series of campuses, each of which focused on a different period and aspect of American landscape history. There was, for example, a Colonial Campus dedicated to the 18th century landscape, which centered on the Mount Vernon Garden; and an American Frontier Campus built around the enhanced Lewis and Clark National Historic Trail. An American Parks Campus was designed to showcase the styles of the American landscape architects Frederick Law Olmsted and Jens Jensen; and a Contemporary Campus that would follow American landscape design into the 20th century.

One of the first tasks was the removal of a classic English standard, a network of hedges—fat, thin, high, low, and often overgrown—that parceled the landscape into small, disjunct pieces. We sought to give the landscape a more open, American feel, while removing the living walls that obscured breathtaking views of the bucolic Limpley Stoke Valley below the museum's grounds. At the same time we opened up the grounds, knitting together the different features with a coordinated system of paths designed for accessibility for all the visitors to the museum.

Concerns with accessibility of a different sort initiated moving the ticket booth from the museum entrance to the grounds, to prevent traffic from backing up on the adjoining road. Instead, a pair of garden pavilions, designed by Nash Partnership of Bath, England, adjoin the manor house and serve as the museum's main point of ticketing and entry.

Set atop the Marquee Lawn that fronts the house, these now frame the entrance to a garden of American roses, rose cultivars that have played a major role in American garden history, and a hillside overlaid with American shrubs.

Central to the new design was the Winding Way, a "tribute" to a meandering path through flower beds that was a prominent feature of Thomas Jefferson's Monticello. This furnishes a fully accessible means of circling the Great Lawn, linking its various points of interest, and provides an approach to a new sculpted turf-rich amphitheater that has been carved out of the base of the Marquee Lawn.

At the suggestion of the museum's director, Dr. Richard Wendorf, we focused the Winding Way plantings on the New American Garden, pioneered by our firm. The planting was true to the original vision for this two-and-a-half–acre space, in its arrangement of flower plantings along this path, but the beds were transformed into expansive garden vignettes that take strollers through the evolution of our design from the founding of the firm to the present: a more-than-40-year evolution. Visitors first encounter the palette of perennials and grasses, such as sedums, fountain grass, and black-eyed Susans that the founding partners made famous in the early years of the firm. There are also glimpses of the planting style we developed for commissions at the Chicago Botanic Garden, a flash of the New York Botanical Garden's Native Plants Garden, and a nod, in a forest of alliums, to private retreats that we had created.

The transformation of the grounds has turned the garden from an afterthought into an integral part of the museum's mission. Clear evidence of the impact of this redesign is manifested in the new institutional name. Initially known as The American Museum when OvS arrived, the institution now announces itself as The American Museum & Gardens.

OPPOSITE Layered blooms of white-flowered *Allium nigrum* 'Silver Spring' (ornamental onion) overlaid on a ground of purple-flowered *Allium schubertii*, create a visual shimmer in the New American Garden in front of the American Museum & Gardens' Manor House. Seven different types of allium were planted in a tradition of horticultural richness.

RIGHT An aerial photograph shows the new network of accessible paths and gardens, as well as the Manor House, the new twin-entrance pavilions, with the American Rose Garden and the American Shrub Collection, which link to the Winding Way, a series of American gardens, the amphitheater, *left,* and eventually connects to the Mount Vernon Garden, planted as a series of fleur-de-lis.

RIGHT Flanking the path in the foreground is a mix of *Perovskia atriplicifolia* (Russian sage) and *Coreopsis tinctoria* (golden tickseed), interspersed with *Hydrangea arborescens* 'Annabelle' (smooth hydrangea).

RIGHT Deeper into the New American Garden, classic *Allium giganteum* 'Summer Drummer' (giant ornamental onion)–was boldly planted in the thousands.

RIGHT The vista from
the Manor House across
the Marquee Lawn
reveals views of the
Limpley Stoke Valley.

RIGHT *Gaura lindheimeri*
(white gaura) and purple
Verbena bonariensis
(purpletop vervain) fill the
foreground with blue
Nepeta (catmint) across
the path, all shrouded
by the mist rising from
the River Avon, below.

RIGHT In the summer, the sculptural amphitheater accommodates performances as well as providing a playground for tumbling children.

THE ALDERMAN QUAD AT THE UNIVERSITY OF VIRGINIA CHARLOTTESVILLE, VIRGINIA

OPPOSITE The challenge was to create an appropriate landscape to overlay the subterranean extension for the Albert and Shirley Small Special Collections Library, while uniting the disparate elements of the surrounding quad into an harmonious whole.

With its history of involvement by founder Thomas Jefferson, the University of Virginia campus is a national treasure, but also presents a supreme test of the skills of any landscape architect asked to redesign any of its elements. OvS felt honored to be chosen to design the new Alderman Quadrangle, a project on which we collaborated extensively with the Washington, DC-based firm Hartman–Cox Architects.

Our extensive experience integrating lush planting with structure was a perfect fit. The design fronted the Albert and Shirley Small Special Collections Library and expanded the focus to also integrate it with the surroundings.

Alderman Quad is one of the busiest areas of the university campus. Along with the Special Collections Library, it accommodates not only the Alderman Library (the main library for the university), Peabody Hall (home to the Office of the Dean of Students and the Office of Admissions), Monroe Hall (offices for the College of Arts & Sciences), and the main approach to Newcomb Hall, the student union. Located across the street from the West Range of the Academical Village, the core campus, which was designed by founder Thomas Jefferson, Alderman Quad is a highly visible and heavily used area, yet, when we arrived in 2000, the space was disjointed and uncoordinated. The individual buildings, although stylistically harmonious in their use of red brick, white trim, and columns, did not relate to each other.

While dealing with the space over the new extension of the Special Collections Library, we were able to reorganize the Quad. Several flights of steps extending in different directions to overcome the eight feet of grade change were removed and the Quad was regraded to a gentle slope. An esplanade from the Alderman Library includes a series of broad planting beds, which cascade down the length of the newly leveled Quad to unite the grounds into a single landscape that offers universal accessibility.

Planting areas were established in front of the Special Collections Library. As we were aware that students used the campus primarily in the fall, winter, and early spring, we planned its plantings accordingly. White roses provide red hips in the fall and evergreen *Liriope muscari* (liriope) and *Nandina domestica* (dwarf heavenly bamboo) were planted as ground cover in the beds of the central spine. Other seasonal attractions included crabapples and oakleaf hydrangea, whose bold green leaves turn brilliant shades of crimson, purple, orange, gold, and bronze in the autumn. Winter with its evegreen plantings presents a different graphic view. Thomas Jefferson, a noted plantsman, would have approved.

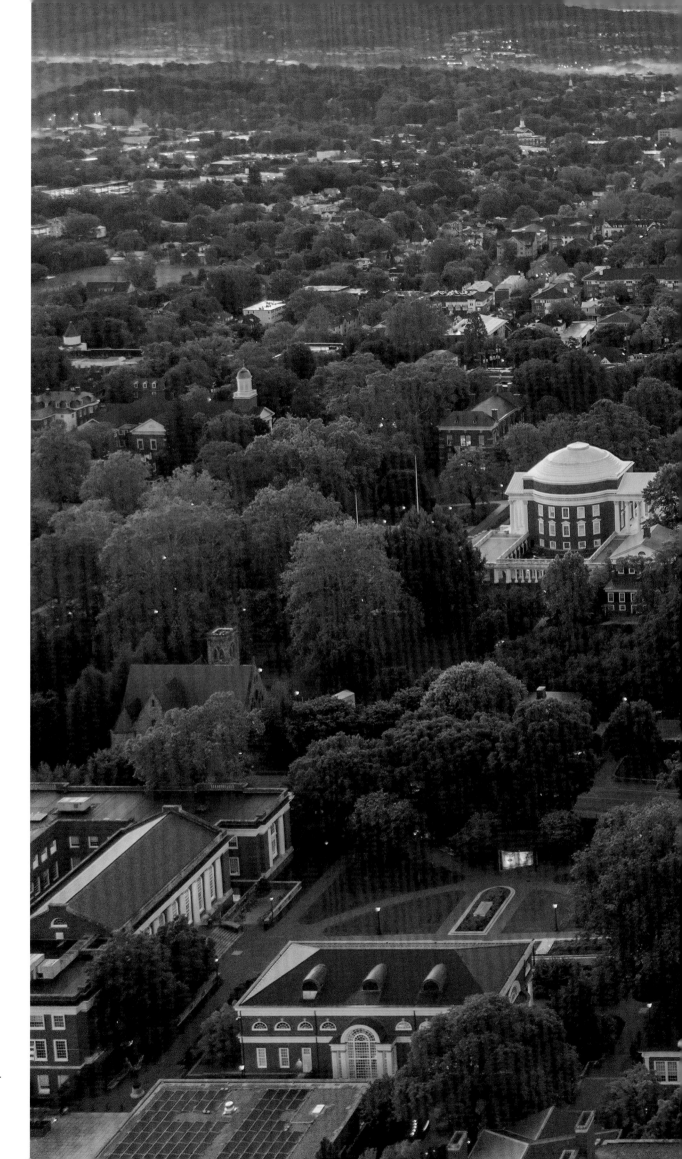

RIGHT The Alderman Quad is situated within 150 feet of the Thomas Jefferson Rotunda and the Academical Village.

RIGHT Regrading the Quad to accommodate universal accessibility necessitated installing five feet of fill around a majestic *Fraxinus pennsylvanica* (green ash). Shale was used to preserve its roots: The lightweight and porous material allows air and water to penetrate to the tree's roots.

THE NATIVE PLANT GARDEN AT THE NEW YORK BOTANICAL GARDEN
THE BRONX, NEW YORK

Although it occupies a site of just three-and-a-half acres, this garden's creation was a considerable undertaking. The ambitious goal was to create a celebration of the northeastern United States using native flora that would both educate the public with its biodiversity and inspire gardeners with its beauty and functionality. Another consideration was that native plants, which in general do not have a long history of domestication, tend to be very habitat specific, requiring specific soil types, moisture, and degrees of sunlight to flourish. As a result, design and planting had to be preceded by an intensive site analysis, involving collaboration with soil scientists, ecologists, engineers, and horticulturists from the NYBG staff. The resulting garden, which involved the planting of 100,000 trees, shrubs, and perennials, was the product of five years of collaborations.

This was not the first native plants garden on the site, as displays of wildflowers and native plants had been cultivated there since the 1930s. But the earlier gardens had reflected the thinking of an era that viewed wild plants as specimens to be assembled into a kind of botanical zoo, planted into miniature recreations of habitats that had been too small and artificial to function ecologically. The plants did not coalesce into actual communities, and maintenance devolved into an ongoing battle to contain the more vigorous, weedy species. The focus on habitat recreation had also distracted from the beauty of the plants and visitors had responded by largely staying away.

Our in-depth analysis identified many opportunities for different kinds of vegetation. The garden's site is defined by a pair of parallel ridges, one wooded, the other open, with a small, artificial stream running down a small valley between them. This rather dramatic variation in natural conditions creates a diversity of zones ranging from "xeric" or upland dry woodland to "mesic," or moderately moist meadow and outright wetlands in the low-lying areas.

A key part of transforming the site into a visually appealing garden lay in playing up the water feature. We expanded what had been little more than a meandering trickle into a series of three pools that spilled one into the

other. This centered the landscape, endowing it with drama, while also serving a very real environmental role. Fed mainly by rainwater collected in a series of underground cisterns, the water feature serves to cleanse the runoff of the silt and pollutants that it had collected on its journey down the adjacent slopes. We fed the water first through a constructed wetland at the head of the network of pools and then ran it through sand and gravel filters. At the outlet of the pools, the water is pumped back up to the head of the pools, to maintain the flow without the need for constant inputs. When storms provide an excess of water, it drains down through another wetland, where it continues to be naturally filtered and cleansed before emptying into the nearby Bronx River.

Our planting of the new garden was emphatically diverse, including some 450 different trees, shrubs, wildflowers, ferns, and grasses drawn from the whole of northeastern North America from New Brunswick to Virginia and west to the Mississippi River. These plantings were carefully synchronized to the conditions within the site, and interwoven into a brilliant tapestry of color, texture, and fragrance. Conceived of as an evolving rather than a static composition, the plants emerge and bloom at different times throughout the seasons in an ever-changing display, and are finding their own regeneration through self-seeding and natural colonization.

The display works to awaken visitors to the aesthetic as well as to the ecological importance of these indigenous species. An accessible path winds through the landscape, introducing visitors to natural features, from a large, glacially deposited boulder, Split Rock, and outcrops of the native Manhattan schist, then winding down through a display of rare trilliums, ephemeral spring wildflowers and ferns, to a wooden promenade along the water feature made of sustainably grown and harvested black locust lumber.

Validation of the design can be found in the vastly increased number of visitors to the Native Plant Garden, as well as its attraction of a wealth of wildlife, from pollinators to wild turkeys. Nature recognizes this landscape as her own.

OPPOSITE Decking of native black-locust lumber surrounds the water feature in the Native Plant Garden, an example of a weather-resistant, environmentally friendly alternative to the endangered tropical hardwoods commonly used in North American landscape construction.

RIGHT Existing features of the site include the glacial moraine erratic boulder, Split Rock, that was linked and incorporated into the garden experience along with accessible paths.

RIGHT The water feature in autumn reflects the coloring of the tree and shrub foliage, giving the scene a sylvan atmosphere that can persuade visitors they are far removed from the heart of the busy city.

RIGHT Designed to be beautiful in all seasons, the Native Plant Garden takes on a special fascination in midwinter, when snowfall erases all the colors and reveals the bones of the landscape in all of its monochromatic complexity and severity.

Context is a central concern in the design of any gathering place that is part of a larger complex and is especially true of an environment with as strong a character as the monument area in our nation's capital, including the landscape around the Martin Luther King, Jr., National Memorial. The design, conceptualized by the San Francisco, California-based ROMA Design Group, was further developed by the Washington, DC, architectural firm McKissack & McKissack. The four-acre site offers views of both the Franklin Delano Roosevelt and Thomas Jefferson memorials that extend in a crescent along the shore of Washington, DC's Tidal Basin. All around the Tidal Basin is the famed collection of *Prunus* x *yedoensis* (Japanese Yoshino cherry) originally donated by the city of Tokyo more than a century ago. Every spring, when the trees erupt into bloom, Washington celebrates with the National Cherry Blossom Festival.

The decision to make cherry trees the dominant element of the Martin Luther King, Jr., landscape was obvious. Even so, we put our own twist on the design. Along with the 171 Yoshino cherry trees now arranged throughout the site, the planting included 11 *Prunus subhirtella* 'Autumnalis' (Edo Higan cherry), another Japanese cherry tree that, as its cultivar name suggests, blooms not only in the spring, but again in the fall.

Ulmus americana (American elm) of a Dutch elm disease–resistant cultivar 'Princeton' shade the pedestrian walkways at the perimeter of the landscape, providing welcome shelter from the sun in the summer. Ecologically, elms are a floodplain tree whose roots can flourish in poorly aerated soils, which is necessary in a setting such as this one, with compacted, damp soils. But here, the elms' growth has been enhanced by planting them into modular suspended pavement cells that provide each tree with more than 1,000 cubic feet of loam soil complete with a built-in drainage system that helps storm water to infiltrate the soil and prevents water stagnation. As the elms mature, their leafy embrace adds further dignity to this solemn site.

While honoring the site's context, however, we also worked to create a distinctive and dignified setting for the great civil rights leader's memorial. The design team instilled a note of solemnity with an abundant use of evergreens: 161 compact *Abelia* x *grandiflora* 'Rose Creek' (pink abelia), more than 500 spreading *Taxus* x *media* 'Green Wave' (Anglojap yew), and 37,000 *Liriope muscari* 'Big Blue' (liriope). If the evergreens should become oppressive and dull, a wealth of flowering shrubs and perennials were also introduced into the landscape. In addition to the abelias, which bear fragrant white and pink flowers in summer, the shrub planting included dwarf *Itea virginica* 'Little Henry' (Virginia sweetspire), which sprouts spikes of lightly fragrant white flowers in late spring, and *Jasminum nudiflorum* (winter jasmine), whose arching green stems bear yellow flowers in late winter before the leaves emerge. Perennials add notes of white, blue, and yellow throughout the growing season. The movement of visitors through the landscape is also an essential element of the design of any place of assembly. Curving paths extend from the statue of King that is the central focus of the memorial, inviting visitors onto a thoughtful stroll.

OPPOSITE The delicacy of the cherry blossoms contrasts dramatically with the massive granite monoliths of the Martin Luther King, Jr., Memorial. The flowering peaks usually around the first week of April, suitably memorializing the April 4th anniversary of the Civil Rights leader's death.

RIGHT A curving path through Yoshino cherry trees in glorious bloom invites the visitor to the central plaza of the Martin Luther King, Jr., Memorial. Half-hidden by the blossoms is the statue of the slain civil rights leader, which faces across the Tidal Basin toward the Thomas Jefferson and Franklin Delano Roosevelt memorials, suggesting the arc followed by America's quest for freedom.

RIGHT Four acres of gardens surround the architectural center of the memorial, Master Lei Yixin's *A Stone of Hope*. The gardens help integrate the sculpture into the landscape and imbue what could be a sad scene with an air of ever-renewed vitality.

4

AT THE WATER'S EDGE

The presence of water in a landscape introduces a dynamic feature that is both an opportunity and a challenge. Water reflects the light and the sky, capturing and bringing them into a composition. It moves and changes with the seasons and the weather. The murmur of it falling or running creates a soothing sound track that affects people on a visceral level. It also appeals to the eye. A simple water addition, such as a fountain or pool, in even the smallest garden, offers an arresting visual tableau.

The presence of natural streams, rivers, lakes, and oceans in a landscape is a tremendous asset. Yet even created water bodies bring with them a need for heightened ecological sensitivity and responsibilities. Leaving a landscape system at the water's edge healthier than when we found it requires skillful management.

Not the least of water's impact on a landscape is its effect on the immediate ecology. As a fundamental requirement for plant growth, the presence of abundant moisture encourages more vegetation and a greater concentration of wildlife. A body of water also generates a microclimate, absorbing and retaining the sun's heat, to keep its surroundings warmer in the fall and winter than nearby waterless regions. As anyone who has enjoyed the beach in the summer knows, the presence of a large body of water can have a tempering effect on the seasonal heat. This makes the water's edge an attractive destination and creates an opportunity for the adventurous planter who can thus grow flora that elsewhere could not weather the extremes of winter and summer.

Water, one of our most sensitive resources, is easily degraded by careless treatment. It is in the character of a natural waterway to be transient. The water comes from somewhere outside the control of the designer or landowner, and, after traveling through, leaves the property for another destination.

Water systems intersect with terrestrial ones in ways defined by the body of water itself. There is tremendous power in water, whether it is stirred to movement by wind, current, tide, or ice. If not dealt with intelligently and scientifically, it will lead to erosion of and damage to the littoral zone, the fragile lands close to the shore. How we confront this problem depends on the local circumstances. We may armor the shoreline with a retaining wall, or revetment, or perhaps with intensive planting. We may have to restore the shallows, dredging and stabilizing them with emergent plants, recreating the natural spawning area for fish.

On a practical level, the presence of water in a landscape nearly always brings jurisdictional involvement from agencies as varied as the US Army Corps of Engineers to state and local governments. Achieving a design solution that is rooted in science, historically effective, and beautifully executed, requires immersive study of a site's geology, ecology, and geography, which we undertake before beginning any project. Understanding the context leads to design that not only makes the most of the site but also helps us to avoid problems before they arise.

All this demands sophisticated artistry. When successful, the result seems inevitable, as if the landscape has assumed a form it was always meant to take.

OPPOSITE Located on a small island on Long Island Sound, the century-old home is delightfully secluded, connected to the mainland by only a causeway. Working with the New York-based John B. Murray, Architect, and the New York-based interior design firm Bunny Williams Interior Design, OvS fit all the amenities the client desired into the narrow terraces—much like assembling a jigsaw puzzle. Native coastal plantings complement the locally quarried granite used on the terrace that alluded to not only the granite walls of the house, but also to the rocky shoreline.

RIGHT Capturing striking views of Delaware's Silver Lake and the Atlantic Ocean, this residence, a collaboration with Robert M. Gurney, a Washington, DC-based architectural firm, exemplifies the definition of being at the "Water's Edge."

RIGHT A residential garden in Kittery, Maine, overlooks the Piscatauqua River and Spruce Creek.

RIGHT An iconic Hamptons beach house, locally known as the "Kennedy House," reflecting its previous owners, was revitalized by a long-time client. OvS developed a palette tolerant of the windy conditions and salt air, including *Ammophila breviligulata* (American beachgrass) on the dune, and meadow grasses on the leeward side of the house.

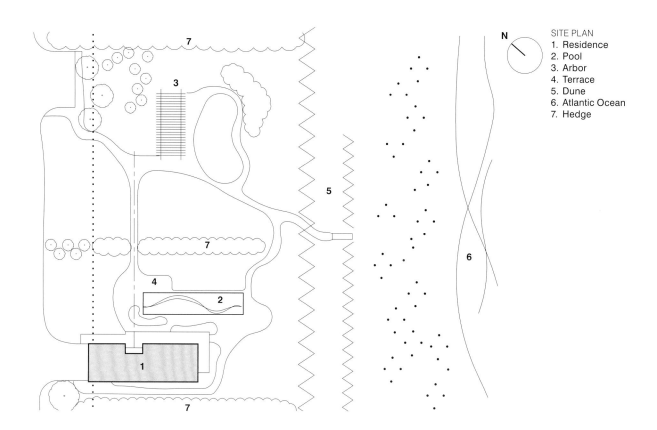

SITE PLAN
1. Residence
2. Pool
3. Arbor
4. Terrace
5. Dune
6. Atlantic Ocean
7. Hedge

Multiple commissions from our clients highlight our commitment to our work and the practice of our craft. In this case, this was our third commission, when our client purchased an adjoining beachfront house that blocked the ocean view from her newly moved residence. The client tore down the obtrusive house and asked us to landscape the new beachfront property. It adjoined the property with Boardwalk House, a small modern structure designed by Demetriades + Walker of Lakeville, Connecticut, that had been designed when the main residence had been moved to avoid being destroyed by a major storm.

Simply erasing the boundary between the old beachfront property and the new one would have left the structure out of scale with the landscape. We decided to integrate the new property with the old by extending an existing, Japanese-inspired fence along the road in front of the new addition, and by using the same Roxbury granite slabs for paving that we had used around Boardwalk House. The two landscapes, however, were to be treated as separate garden rooms, and an existing hedge that had been planted between them was left intact.

Ordinarily, hedges are not a part of the OvS horticultural vocabulary. But in the Hamptons, privet hedges are a hallmark of the landscape, and these were hedges with a difference, as we allowed the sea wind to 'trim' them so that they naturally followed the inclination of the Boardwalk House. The client preferred this approach, as she liked the white flowers that cover them in the summer and the black seedheads that appear in the fall.

No trees were planted in or near the new addition, as we didn't want to interrupt the sweeping view to the ocean. Instead, we adapted the ground-hugging contours of the natural dune vegetation, using native perennials and grasses as well as *Yucca filamentosa* (yucca), *Limonium carolinianum* (sea lavender), and cultivars of *Schizachyrium scoparium* (little bluestem). *Allium sphaerocephalon* (drumstick allium) to satisfy the client's love of the color purple. Large boulders were set around the new dune garden to frame views and along paths, to provide visual punctuation, planting the stones on end with their bases buried in the ground in a Japanese style. As seen here, naturalism in the garden is not incompatible with aesthetics.

RIGHT The verticality of this picket fence, inspired by an OvS trip to Japan with the client, is complemented by *Calamagrostis* x *acutiflora* (feather reed grass) and the leafy *Hibiscus moscheutos* (swamp rose mallow), which blooms later in the summer. The path is interplanted with *Sedum spurium* 'John Creech.' *Allium gigantium* 'Lucy Ball' (giant ornamental onion) are set against a backdrop of natural privet, which is ubiquitous in the Hamptons.

RIGHT A meandering path of Roxbury granite, the same stone used for the Brooklyn Bridge, leads to the ocean. The designed dunescape was meant to blur the natural and the designed landscape, using plants native to the area, along with adaptive species. *Ammophila breviligulata* (American beachgrass) and *Schizachyrium scoparium* (little bluestem) in the foreground mix with *Yucca filamentosa* (yucca) and *Eryngium yuccifolium* (rattlesnake master) to provide texture.

RIGHT Responding to the client's love of purple, a profusion of *Verbena bonariensis* 'Lollipop' (purpletop vervain), which blooms all summer long, adds to the effect of the allium of a similar hue, which blooms in the spring. Sweeps of *Panicum virgatum* (switchgrass) and *Rudbeckia hirta* (Black-eyed Susan) are set against the backdrop of the natural privet hedge, whose aerodynamic shape—lower on the left and higher on the right—was created by ocean breezes. The perennials and grasses, juxtaposed against a rigid background, are an OvS signature.

RIGHT Boulders, used in the site's prior shoreline revetment, were artistically arranged in the garden, in contrast to the planting. Lovingly named the Oyster, the boulder is framed with *Sedum spurium* 'John Creech' and *Salvia* x *sylvestris* 'Mainacht' (wood sage). An array of vertical grasses such as *Sporobolus heterolepis* (prairie dropseed) and *Lupinus polyphyllus* (lupine) provided a background for the vignette.

RIGHT Boulders accent the garden throughout, looking from the dunescape to the main house designed by the East Hampton, New York, firm Zwirko Ortmann & Hugo Architects. At center, *Opuntia humifusa* (Eastern prickly pear), the only native cactus on the East Coast, is nestled among five different species of ornamental onion.

174

The intersection of two different habitats makes design at the water's edge particularly challenging. It has been especially so in the case of the Chicago Botanic Garden, where land and water thoroughly interpenetrate in its 385-acre complex of lakes, lagoons, and islands. This complication also creates tremendous opportunities, however, as OvS has proven in the many projects it has designed and implemented for the Botanic Garden.

One notable complication is that the landscapes and gardens at the Botanic Garden have no "back." They do not back up against a wall, hedge, or woods, and are instead equally visible from every angle—from the land, but also from bridges and other islands. So the designer must work in 360 degrees, creating a landscape in the round.

The Chicago Botanic Garden's site comes with some practical strictures as well. As mentioned previously, it functions as flood control for the adjacent Skokie River, absorbing and then gradually releasing storm water surges. To ensure that this capability isn't diminished, the Botanic Garden is under the supervision of the U.S. Army Corps of Engineers as well as state and local jurisdictions. In the projects, we worked in coordination with not only personnel from the Botanic Garden but also with the Corps of Engineers, local jurisdictions, and garden stakeholders.

The initial focus was the Great Basin, a circular body of water that is the geographic center and programmatic focus of the Botanic Garden campus. Several gardens already adorned its shores. Our brief was to integrate these distinct landscapes and to improve pedestrian circulation.

Integration was achieved by reworking the collective shore. This had consisted of turfed slopes running down to the water's edge, a solution which had proven not only visually abrupt but also problematic in that it allowed the action of ice in wintertime to undercut and erode the shore.

We regraded the shore to a shallower slope so that it merged more gradually with the water. The underwater edges were armored with rock to resist the battering of the ice, and then planted with emergent species such as

Iris versicolor (blue flag iris) and Sagittaria latifolia (broadleaf arrowhead) to bind together the land and water interface. At the same time, the outline of the shore was re-sculpted to create a more natural-seeming meander.

As a collection of islands, the Botanic Garden presents special challenges to visitor circulation. Bridges were a key to enhancing what may be thought of as the choreography of this landscape, to shaping the experience and directing the visitor to selected views. We had already installed two such structures—the low and rhythmic Serpentine Bridge, and the taller, more classical Arched Bridge. Both connected the central Education Island with Evening Island to the south, completing a circular path around the periphery of the Great Basin. To these, we added a third, Trellis Bridge, which connects the eastern shore of Evening Island with the Daniel F. and Ada L. Rice Plant Conservation Science Center. Fans of cables stretched from either end of the Trellis Bridge to enable vines to grow up and envelop its entrances, literally tethering the bridge to the landscape.

Elevated above the ground so that its footprint would not diminish the water-absorptive capacity of the landscape, the Daniel F. and Ada L. Rice Plant Conservation Science Center was topped with a 16,000-square-foot green roof. Intended to capture the storm water that falls on it, this roof was also designed as a demonstration garden that has expanded the usual green roof flora of sedums to include a broad range of native and adapted shrubs, perennials, and grasses.

A final aspect of all this design that is a hallmark for our firm, it was conceived of in four seasons. This was especially important in Chicago, where winters are long and the Botanic Garden cannot appeal to visitors with only warm weather blooms. Views were framed with trees such as oaks that retain their leaves into the fall and even through the winter, and complemented with shrubs such as the Cornus sericea (red-twig dogwood) whose vivid bark emerges visually when the foliage falls away in the fall. Defying ordinary horticultural practice, perennials and grasses are left uncut in the fall, to furnish a tawny, structured cover throughout the dormant season.

OPPOSITE The Serpentine Bridge was inspired by the graceful meander of Japanese stepping-stones as they traverse a pond. The curves of the bridge are punctuated by colonies of aquatic plants that can be viewed from above by those crossing the bridge.

RIGHT *Malus* 'Donald Wyman' (crabapple) trees were planted around the Great Basin to provide a joyous explosion of seasonal color.

OVERLEAF Planting that can delight through four seasons is essential at a public garden that aspires to attract visitors year 'round. From spring, *top left*, through summer, *top right*, fall, *bottom left*, and winter, *bottom right*, the shores of the Chicago Botanic Garden's Great Basin offer a succession of colors and blooms—from the white blossoms of spring's crabapples, through the roses of high summer, the russets and golds of the autumn grasses, to the snowscapes and skeletal browns of midwinter.

RIGHT The 120-foot-long Arch Bridge connects Evening Island and Education Island at their respective high points, arching up to allow the water below to flow undisturbed. *Salix babylonica* (weeping willow) overhang the bridge at each end, creating a sense of mystery and deferring enjoyment of the water views until the visitor reaches the bridge's center.

RIGHT Careful sculpting of the Great Basin's underwater terrain and special plantings were required to give the aquatic vegetation a dynamic yet natural appearance. The plants used include *Acorus calamus* 'Variegatus' (sweet flag), *Carex comosa* (bristly sedge), *Iris pseudacorus* (yellow flag), *Juncus effusus* (soft rush), *Juncus torreyi* (Torrey's rush), and *Lobelia cardinalis* (cardinal flower).

RIGHT The Trellis Bridge was the third of the three bridges that were designed for the Botanic Garden. Connecting Evening Island with the southern edge of the garden, it was conceived of as a garden 'trellis,' allowing plants to climb out on its cables to tether the bridge to the opposing shores. Following a sinuous path, the bridge rises and falls to pick up the topography of the land forms.

OVERLEAF LEFT Stone blocks at the right of the Daniel F. and Ada L. Rice Plant Conservation Science Center serve as visual registration of the heights reached by flood waters in 50- and 100-year storms.

OVERLEAF RIGHT
The 38,000-square-foot Daniel F. and Ada L. Rice Plant Conservation Science Center is the nexus for the garden's research efforts. In addition to two 8,000-square-foot green roofs, the LEED Gold facility provides classrooms, laboratories, and interactive displays and is the headquarters for masters and doctoral programs in plant biology and conservation.

PREVIOUS PAGES
OvS designers worked
with the Chicago
Botanic Garden to
install an experimental
effort of green roof
plants on top of the
Daniel F. and Ada L. Rice
Plant Conservation
Science Center.

RIGHT In the foreground
are evaluation gardens
established to test
different plants in varying
depths of soil over a
five-year period. On
the left are plantings of
sedums and other
adapted plants from
around the world; on
the right is a test garden
of native species. In the
rear are display gardens
where visitors may
view the performance
of complexes of
selected plants.

RIGHT Winters are long in Chicago, but it is a season of great beauty at the Botanic Garden, as seen in this view of the Serpentine Bridge.

SPIRIT OF THE SOUND DARIEN, CONNECTICUT

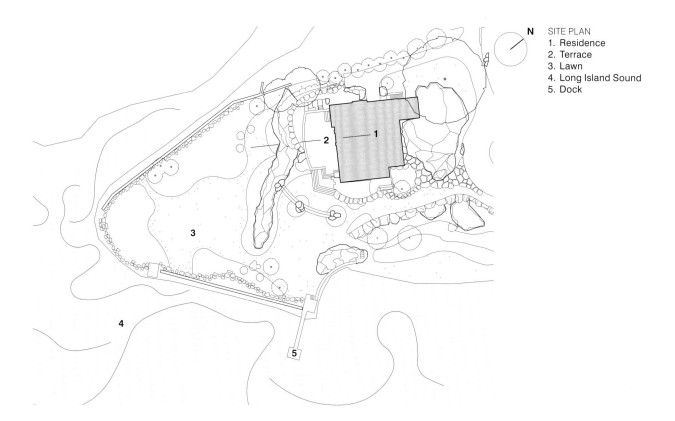

N

SITE PLAN
1. Residence
2. Terrace
3. Lawn
4. Long Island Sound
5. Dock

OPPOSITE Planting began at the house on this seaside landscape with adapted grasses such as *Panicum amarum* 'Dewey Blue' (blue switchgrass), perennials such as *Lavandula angustifolia* 'Provence' (English lavender) and *Artemisia ludoviciana* 'Silver King' (wormwood), and was carried on down in an expanse of colors and textures to below the high-tide line.

A property that came equipped with a notable history, the expansive site on Long Island Sound had been the home of Charles and Anne Morrow Lindbergh for several decades. Located in the exclusive Tokeneke neighborhood of Darien, Connecticut, the property has sweeping views of Scott Cove. Subdivided and sold after Anne Morrow Lindbergh's death in 2001, it was re-assembled by our clients and Austin Patterson Disston, an architecture firm in Southport, Connecticut. OvS was asked to reintegrate the two lots, creating a more hospitable but natural setting for the house.

The site is ruggedly handsome—a rocky point carved by the glaciers of the last ice age—but also challenging. The project began by securing the interface of land and water and installing a stone revetment to stabilize nearly 1,000 linear feet of shoreline—conducted in coordination with the Connecticut State Department of Environmental Protection, a collaboration with which we are adept, due to our numerous coastal projects.

After the revetment was in place, we made judicious use of planting the shallow, tidal land beyond the revetment with masses of *Spartina alterniflora* (native cordgrass), and *Spartina patens* (saltmeadow cordgrass). An existing seawall at the apex of the point was enhanced by capping it with a cut local granite coping, giving it a more finished appearance. We collaborated with the architect to renovate an existing fishing/boathouse, turning it into a pergola from which to experience the landscape and enjoy the views across the Cove to Long Island Sound.

To re-integrate the former lots, we installed paths of turf and granite flagstones connecting the two areas, and

carried the plantings of native and adapted perennials such as the *Hibiscus moscheutos* (swamp rose mallow) and *Perovskia atriplicifolia* (Russian sage) across the landscape in a single, coordinated complex. To satisfy the need of this young family for play space we included swaths of lawn, punctuated sparingly with boulders of native Connecticut granite. Granite retaining walls, of cut stone adjacent to the house, and of more rustic construction as the land dropped toward the shore, rooted the residence while also creating a transition from a refined, manmade landscape to something more natural and indigenous.

The planting reinforced this progression to the natural, while also serving to soften the rocky site. Installed with characteristic bold flair, ornamental grasses such as *Calamagrostis* x *acutiflora* 'Karl Foerster' (feather reed grass) and *Panicum amarum* 'Dewey Blue' (blue switchgrass) were mixed with stalwart perennials. Brushed across the landscape in irregular drifts, these plantings created a meadow-like landscape on what had been a somewhat barren headland. Because they were selected for their adaptability to a coastal environment, these plants have flourished with a minimum of care.

Completing this seaside residential project involved a balancing act of respecting the historic nature of the landscape, and of preserving the existing structures while serving the needs of the new residents. For this, our extensive experience with historic landscapes was a great asset. Both the integration of the house into the natural setting and the transitions from the domesticated to the wild within the landscape, reflect the special sensitivity of the firm.

196

RIGHT Every site poses its unique challenges. This one, with its exposed location and thin, rocky soil, demanded a drought- and salt-tolerant flora. *Juniperus virginiana* (Eastern red cedar), upper right, was a legacy of the Lindbergh residence. The grasses, such as the tawny *Calamagrostis* x *acutiflora* 'Karl Foerster' (feather reed grass), lower right, and the *Sedum spectabile* 'Herbstfreude' (Autumn Joy stonecrop), *middle ground*, right, were our additions.

RIGHT A border of
Hibiscus moscheutos
(swamp rose mallow)
borders a clamshell
path and serves as the
backdrop to the view.
As its common name
suggests, this plant
is well adapted to
waterside locations.

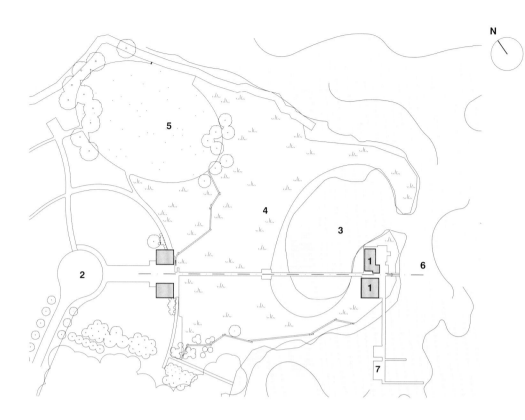

N

SITE PLAN
1. Hosting Houses
2. Forecourt
3. Tidal Pool
4. Meadow
5. Lawn
6. Coan River
7. Dock

A site with such a unique character is rewarding and intriguing for the designer, but often also challenging. The 12-acre peninsula and attached tidal pond reaching out into the confluence of the Coan and Potomac Rivers in Virginia's Northern Neck region is a quintessential example of this. The site offers spectacular views, but also a windswept location bathed with salt spray from every storm, which puts constraints on the type of planting it could support. The area had a history of agricultural use, which had degraded the soil, followed by industrial exploitation, as it had been the site of an oyster-shucking plant.

We began by bringing in topsoil to strategically invigorate the depleted earth. Afterward, we reinforced an existing woodland along the peninsula's northern side to serve as a screen, a backdrop, and a windbreak for the landscape and the house. A variety of arborists concluded that tree plantings would not survive the exposed conditions, but we succeeded by installing an irregular belt of young *Pinus taeda* (loblolly pine) that are native to this coastal region. These have flourished and provide a sturdy backdrop to an elegant grove of *Magnolia virginiana* (sweetbay magnolia), which, as the botanical name suggests, are also indigenous to the region. We decided to use only native plants to enhance the natural aspect of the landscape, placing them in an aesthetic rather than strictly naturalistic arrangement.

Working with the Washington, DC, firm of Overmyer

Architects, the clients' original plan had been to locate the main residence at the eastern edge of the site, the point of the peninsula, but they were so taken with the result of the installation of a guest cottage at the outer edge of the tidal pool that they decided to use that as their home. Accessible only by a lengthy boardwalk and bridge, the residence took the form of a pair of twinned structures that were set on pilings, both to raise them above floodwater surges and to minimize the impact on the fragile tidal habitat.

In this way, the main part of the peninsula became a sort of expansive, informal forecourt and entertainment area. The approach road was lined with an allée of *Juniperus virginiana* (Eastern red cedar) and ended in a turnaround surrounded by a circular meadow whose grasses and flowers were selected for compact height so that this area could be used for parking during parties. Again, indigenous species such as *Eragrostis spectabilis* (purple love grass), *Bouteloua gracilis* (blue grama grass), and *Liatris pilosa* (shaggy blazing star) were selected.

A tennis court was set into the edge of an existing woodland and screened with groves of sweetbay magnolia and masses of seashore shrubs. The land stepping down to the water and the wetlands was planted with broad-brushed stands of refined cultivars of native grasses, such as *Schizachyrium scoparium* 'Blue Heaven' (little bluestem) and *Panicum virgatum* 'Rehbraun' (switchgrass) mixed with compatible perennials.

RIGHT The twin guest cottages frame and anchor the entrance to the bridge across the wetland. The reinforced woodland provides a visual backdrop and shelter from north winds. The young *Pinus taeda* (loblolly pine) trees planted to supplement the existing vegetation have not only survived despite the exposed site, but thrived.

RIGHT The switchgrass is highlighted with dashes of white-flowered *Eupatorium maculatum* 'Bartered Bride' (spotted Joe Pye weed), and the outsized pink blossoms of *Hibiscus moscheutos* 'Plum Crazy' (swamp rose mallow) during the summer in the meadow at the edge of the tidal pond.

RIGHT When evening falls, the residence is silhouetted against the sunset and the confluence of the Potomac and Coan Rivers, LED lights pick out the structure of the bridge across the tidal pool and the pier that is attached to the house.

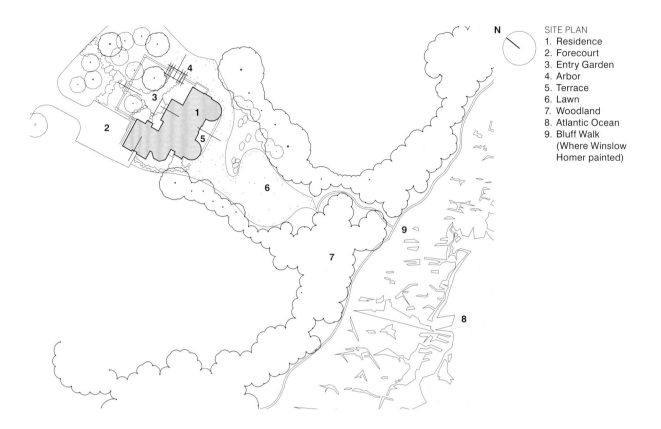

SITE PLAN
1. Residence
2. Forecourt
3. Entry Garden
4. Arbor
5. Terrace
6. Lawn
7. Woodland
8. Atlantic Ocean
9. Bluff Walk
   (Where Winslow
   Homer painted)

OPPOSITE Fashioned from driftwood, a bench by the sculptor Ben Forgey, Jr., strikes an appropriately maritime note for this garden by the sea.

The one-time home of artist Winslow Homer, this iconic Maine seaside community is one in which the client had been spending summers since childhood. A young and growing family was the catalyst in establishing a residence. The original house designed by the late architect Elliott Rosenblum on a one-acre lot atop a seaside bluff was purchased, and the decision was made to replace it with new construction. We had designed the landscape around the clients' home in Greenwich, Connecticut, and they turned to us for assistance again.

The commission was shaped by a few critical dynamics. First was the setting on the edge of Saco Bay, which offered dramatic ocean views that, while an invaluable asset, required a strong hand on the part of the designers for the landscape to provide adequate counterbalance. Second was the climate, with the exposed, northern setting. A recent covenant within the community required the construction of the house and landscape to be carried out between Labor Day and Memorial Day. This requirement dictated a tight, disciplined schedule.

An entirely different style of landscape design was employed here than had been in the client's more southerly Connecticut home. In Maine, we urged the client to emphasize the regional context and use classic Maine flora and locally sourced materials. For example, the site's stone walls were built with locally sourced glacial cobbles and boulders, and the paths were paved with granite quarried up the coast in Deer Isle. Even the large pots that flanked the entrance were made in Maine potteries.

The landscape was divided into two zones—one

between the house and the road, the other between the house and the bluff's edge. There is a strong tradition in the areas of coastal Maine of visiting between homes on foot or by bicycle, so the distance between the house and road is purposely inviting. Large stone steps fronted on the road, providing easy access into an intimate entry garden. This space was flanked on one side by the garage wing of the new house that was abutted on the other side with a substantial wooden pergola with built-in seating. Instead of turf, the space between the road and the entry garden was planted with *Vaccinium angustifolium* (lowbush blueberry) sod. Within beds of the walled entry garden is a classic Maine garden flora originally popularized by the early 20th-century landscape architect Beatrix Farrand, whose own home and famous garden is located on the coast of Maine and which emphasized cool colors—whites, yellows, and blues—that create an air of serenity.

Planting on the seaward side of the house highlighted a Maine flora of a different sort. The trees that frame the space are white: *Picea glauca* (white spruce) and *Picea omorika* (Serbian spruce), chosen to harmonize with the indigenous forest. The porch that provided seaside views is embraced with a band of *Carex elata* (tufted sedge) to create a foreground to the ocean. Around the edge of the sweeping lawn, along the crest of the bluff, we planted elements of coastal Maine meadows. *Monarda didyma* (scarlet beebalm), mustard-yellow *Rudbeckia hirta* (Black-eyed Susans), *Solidago* spp. (goldenrod), and blush pastel *Lupinus perennis* (wild lupine) that are assertive enough to hold vistas that might have come from Homer's brush.

RIGHT Locally crafted bowls by Lunaform planted with *Pelargonium tomentosum* (peppermint-scented geranium) cap cobblestone pillars, providing an aromatic invitation to the entryway garden with its cool colors set off by delicate foliar textures.

RIGHT Climbing vines and billowing perennials accentuate the lines of the locally quarried granite path and elegant timber-framed pergola.

RIGHT **Pegged together from salvaged cypress timbers, the pergola is a demonstration of fine craftsmanship.**

RIGHT Vistas are judiciously dispensed. The evergreen screening of spruces has been used to direct the eye down through the back garden to the ocean beyond.

RIGHT Hot colors, such as the brilliant scarlet blossoms of this *Monarda didyma* (scarlet beebalm), enliven the back garden and compete for attention with the spectacular ocean views.

Set on the bank of the Anacostia River, not only is this landscape at the water's edge, but it is also intimately involved with water, which is integrated into every aspect of the design.

The headquarters of DC Water, a sewer and water utility serving the District of Columbia and several suburban neighborhoods, has both a storied past and a resilient future. On the site, both above and below grade, are the vestiges of 19th- and 20th-century infrastructures. A new, sinuous building, designed by the Washington, DC, office of the SmithGroup, the facility echoes the riverine landscape and encases an existing sewage pumping station. The LEED Platinum building leverages a wastewater thermal recovery system for its heating and cooling.

Our proposal embraced the utility's vision for sustainability by allowing the landscape to demonstrate environmentally enlightened water management. The design solution is exemplary of what a sustainable design truly means in an urban environment, both in the way it is built and the purposes it serves. This was not an easy assignment. While the headquarters was new, the landscape was not. In addition to the preservation of the sewage pumping station, the ground was undergirded with pipes, some more than a century old, which drain much of the District of Columbia. Because of the presence of the pipes, newer landscape methodologies such as soil penetration were impossible. Also, the site as a whole was largely impermeable and would shed any precipitation. Without innovative storm water solutions, an untenable quantity of surface runoff would easily make its way to the adjacent river. Even adding soil to the site was problematic. There was a strict limit as to how much fill we could deposit on the site, since too heavy a load might shift and rupture the numerous old and fragile pipes.

The design team took a systemic approach to the site, capitalizing on inherent and unique opportunities. For the landscape, the site closely resembles a green roof design that relies on storm water sequestration. Fortunately, we had in-depth knowledge and experience with green roofs. Green roofs are designed to grow plants and trap storm water in layers of growing media, overlaid on an impermeable surface. We proposed not only capping the headquarters building with a green roof but treating the whole landscape in this way.

Our experience with green roofs extends back to 1975, when we installed the Federal Reserve Building landscape over an existing parking garage. Subsequently, in addition to other such projects, we had completed the green roof on the Daniel F. and Ada L. Rice Plant Conservation Center Science Center at the Chicago Botanic Garden. Further to eliminating the storm water runoff, we wanted the landscape to be a teaching tool, a demonstration of how to reintegrate storm water into the urban environment—from collection to filtering it and even capitalizing on it as a resource.

The new building includes a nearly half-acre elevated roof garden that recalls the verdant Anacostia Hills in the distance. While the roof retains much of the water that falls on it, any excess drains to planting beds in front of the building and then feeds into two large underground cisterns. The water collected in this way is used for both flushing toilets in the building and irrigation of the landscape.

Other water that falls is channeled through runnels in the paving then into bioswales, where suspended solids settle out and infiltrate into the shallow soil layers, to be cleansed by the soil microflora. Most of the common specifications for such green infrastructures originated in the western states, where precipitation tends to be less episodic. In the East, the rain and snow tend to come harder and faster. So we made these swales deeper than is customary and we planted them with vegetation from emergent wetlands—areas where roots are liable to be under water for extended periods, but where the soil also periodically dries out.

Elsewhere on the site, we used plants from meadows and shortgrass prairies. These are especially suitable for green roof conditions, as they are adapted to shallow, organic-poor soils, can tolerate windy conditions, and can survive extremes such as flooding and drought. Equally important, such plants also do not have the mass of trees and other woody plants, and neither require as much fill nor impose excessive stress on the underground infrastructure.

Although beautiful and sustainable, the landscape is ephemeral. It comes alive when it rains, embracing the hydrological cycle in a visually arresting and audible way.

OPPOSITE A green roof—a meadow in the sky—serves not only to reduce and cleanse storm water, but also turns this utilitarian structure into an aesthetic experience, and is an arresting introduction to the view of the distant Anacostia Hills.

RIGHT The new DC Water and Sewer Authority (DC HQO) headquarters and its site were conceived of as a single sustainable system. OvS worked with the architects to capture, infiltrate, and cleanse the storm water that falls on the site before it drains into the adjacent Anacostia River.

RIGHT The building's transparent walls blur the division between indoors and out. Water captured on the roof and channeled to the foot of the structure creates opportunities for more moisture-loving plants, such as this scarlet-flowered *Monarda didyma* (scarlet beebalm).

226

RIGHT One of the goals for the rooftop terrace was to restore a token of the natural floodplain vegetation to the industrialized shore of the Anacostia River. At left, *Achillea* 'Moonshine' (yarrow) and *Solidago sphacelata* 'Golden Fleece' (dwarf goldenrod), *Nepeta racemosa* 'Walker's Low' (catmint), and *Spiraea japonica* 'Anthony Waterer' (Japanese spirea) wave in the riparian breeze. The roof terrace was designed to follow the general contour of the adjacent shoreline.

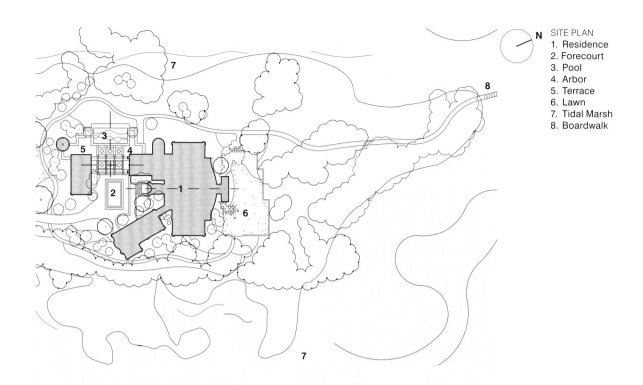

N SITE PLAN
1. Residence
2. Forecourt
3. Pool
4. Arbor
5. Terrace
6. Lawn
7. Tidal Marsh
8. Boardwalk

OPPOSITE Enjoying the fragile lowland ecosystem without damaging it required careful and imaginative design. A curving boardwalk skims over the salt marsh to invite the stroller out to the river beyond.

Located 25 miles southwest of Charleston, South Carolina, Kiawah is a barrier island steeped in a rich maritime history, with nearly 10 miles of sandy beaches, exclusive golf courses, and a cluster of resort communities. Part of South Carolina's low-country landscape, the terrain is flat, but marked by the interpenetration of land and water.

Our clients had purchased an 11-acre parcel on a peninsula in a tidal marsh that runs along the Kiawah River. The property had been logged as part of the early boat trade, but otherwise it remained relatively intact ecologically.

The cedar Shingle Style house, designed by the Norwalk, Connecticut, architecture firm, Shope Reno Wharton, is substantial, yet carefully crafted to rest easily on this relatively narrow spit of land.

Our challenge was to erase the separation of house from land and to nestle the structure into the landscape, and marry the house to the land. We first surrounded the house with strategically placed, elevated terraces and planters, so that the land and vegetation rose to mask the piers on which the house rested. Secondly, we selected plants appropriately scaled to reduce the visual impact of the house. By grouping a series of large specimen trees and shrubs with perennials and ground covers, we created the impression that the house had been built within a mature landscape.

To ensure that the fragile natural habitat would remain undisturbed, the clients put nine beautiful, unspoiled acres of the 11-acre property into conservation status.

RIGHT To withstand the storm surge that accompanies hurricanes, the house was raised almost 20 feet above grade. The installation of native low-country vegetation brought the surrounding landscape into the entry court and gently masked the gap between house and land.

RIGHT A retaining wall, recalling a traditional fencing device in historic English estates called a "ha-ha," defines the boundary between the domesticated landscape near the house and the acreage in conservation—without imposing a visual barrier.

RIGHT The scale of the residence, seen here from the rear, meant that ordinary nursery shrubs would have looked insignificant. Instead, mature-sized specimens were rescued from local landscapes that were undergoing redevelopment. We also selected trees with character—specimens with a curvature to the trunk, for example, that suggested a previous history and gave a more genuine and natural look to the landscape.

236

RIGHT The swimming pool creates an opportunity for relaxation and, when not in use, captures reflections of the surrounding landscape, borrowing its beauty and enhancing its visibility from the house.

RIGHT A cardinal rule: Leave sensitive landscapes in a better state than when we found them. On Kiawah Island, collaborating with the clients to preserve for conservation purposes much of the site, and making sure that added landscape features helped advance preservation of this precious tract of low-country wetland was a priority.

240

5

URBAN RETREATS

It's simply a matter of supply and demand: Open space is more limited in a city, even one with a good park system. Understanding the role and importance of parks, gardens, and general open space in cities is more important than ever.

While a move to an urban center can offer greater employment opportunities, access to healthcare, and culture, it can come at the cost of increased stress, noise, and decreased access to open space, fresh air, and nature. This has proven especially true in recent times, when the refuge of a garden or park is even more essential. Parks and open spaces are not a nicety for urban dwellers, but rather a necessity, and fundamental for healthy cities.

There are myriad environmental and health benefits associated with urban green spaces—a reduction in pollution, storm water mitigation, temperature regulation, and increased biodiversity—all of which add to the quality of life. Plants absorb carbon dioxide, produce oxygen, and help filter airborne and water-borne particulate matter. These spaces also have a direct impact on the health and wellbeing of individuals and communities who use them by facilitating physical activity, relaxation, and refuge from noise. Often centers of social interaction, recreation, and education, green spaces have been proven to reduce health inequalities, extend longevity, and aid in the mitigation of mental illness.

However, the city garden demands a special brand of design. The close scrutiny and the heightened demand on a smaller space make the urban refuge a challenging project. These spaces require enhanced versatility and flexibility—within an arena rife with constraints. In a more expansive suburban or rural landscape, different activities can be assigned their own, parallel spaces. The city garden has no such luxury.

Equally challenging are the myriad subsurface conditions that impact tree and plant health. Urban soils are often devoid of nutrients and heavily compacted. Utility distribution systems; electric, water, gas, and even buildings, form a complex network at various subsurface elevations. Our ethos of working from the ground up has led to high-performance landscapes that champion plant health in a variety of cities and climates.

Horticulturally, these urban sites offer particularly common challenges—extremes in exposure and the fact that urban gardens frequently lie either deep in a canyon of tall buildings with a dearth of sunlight or are on rooftops and other artificially elevated areas that may be as windswept and exposed as a mountain peak. Second, soil depth and volume not only dictate what can initially grow in these harsh environments, but which plants will thrive long-term. Experience and the results of our evaluations offer the best guide as to what plants will flourish, where, and what their needs in any given situation may be.

One common feature of OvS' planting design is its derivation from natural models. Our designs are an aesthetic response to the practical needs and parameters of the site. We work to optimize the ecology of the site, distilling the spirit of natural meadows, prairies, groves, and wetlands into the planting. The allusions to a natural context alleviate the confined, sometimes cramped, nature of the sites. We do not define the garden as a place apart from the outside world. Instead, the garden becomes a true integrated refuge.

OPPOSITE TOP The sleek lines of the terrace, benches, and arbor complement the abundance of *Achillea tomentosa* (woolly yarrow) and *Calamagrostis brachytricha* (Korean feather reed grass) on one of the three roof terraces at the United Therapeutics Corporation. These species thrive in limited soil depths and are tolerant of the dry, windy conditions that prevail high above street level. OvS worked extensively with Washington, DC-based Schick–Goldstein Architects to develop a modern aesthetic for this laboratory in the heart of Silver Spring, Maryland.

OPPOSITE BOTTOM The Hepburn, a luxury residential tower in Washington, DC's Dupont Circle neighborhood, shares a site with the Washington Hilton, an historic hotel, which has a storied past. The hotel has hosted the annual dinners of the White House Correspondents' Association, and was the site of the attempt on President Ronald Reagan's life in 1981. Designed by the architectural firm of Beyer Blinder Belle, which has offices in New York and Washington, DC, in partnership with the Washington, DC, office of developer Lowe Enterprises Real Estate Group, the Hepburn responds to the hemispherical contours of its neighbor, completing the circle begun by one wing of the Hilton. On the street level, OvS tamed a sizable grade change by converting it into a series of concentric, cascading terraces. The area between the hotel and the residential tower, visible from both buildings, is designed to be viewed from above as a painting and from the ground as a mosaic.

RIGHT Nestled in
Washington, DC's historic
Mount Pleasant
neighborhood, the walled
townhouse garden
features diagonal lines
in the hardscape to
lengthen and expand the
modest garden area.
A combination of
layered materials that
include mahogany,
brick, and natural
bluestone creates a
dramatic sense of space.

OPPOSITE The residences
designed by Esocoff
Associates + Weinstein
Studio in Washington, DC,
at 700 Penn in the district's
Capitol Hill neighborhood
feature a courtyard that
can be used for both
intimate and larger
events. The use of richly
textured 'vertical
elements' such as stone,
wood, and trees helps
transition from the larger
space into smaller,
distinct experiences.

RIGHT A dramatic combination of sculpture, architecture, and landscape, Francis Scott Key Park is located on a prominent site overlooking the Potomac River at the Key Bridge entrance to Georgetown in Washington, DC, and is close to the site of Key's home at the time he wrote the American national anthem. The centerpiece is a wisteria-covered circular arbor and terrace of brick, brownstone, and limestone that provides the setting for a bronze bust of Key by the sculptor Betty Mailhouse Dunston.

RIGHT The inspiration for this green roof, in the middle of The Bowery in New York, which is in a 13-story residential tower, designed by New York's Selldorf Architects, was a peregrine falcon's nest. The garden is appropriately lofty— elevated high enough above street level to escape most of the noise, and to take advantage of bird's-eye urban views. Eighteen inches of soil-less growing medium furnishes a floor to the nest, with the medium mounded up deeper to accommodate a *Platanus* x *acerifolia* (London plane tree) that marks the division between the private and common areas. A drift of *Jasminum nudiflorum* (winter jasmine) provides linear mounds of bright yellow flowers in early spring, and two masses of evergreen *Juniperus chinensis* 'Sea Green' (Chinese juniper) frame the planting of the common area. Like a bird's nest, the garden provides a serene retreat removed from the busy cacophony of the street below. To the left is the common space for the condominium residents; to the right, the private garden for the adjacent unit.

In an urban setting, every square foot of open space is precious—particularly when located atop a building. For many years, the 20,000-square-foot rooftop space remained a wasted opportunity. Washington, DC, building-height regulations dictated that the interior penthouse spaces could not be finished and could only be used to house the building's mechanical systems. However, in 2011, a legal change allowed these spaces to be developed. Thanks to our pioneering green roof garden at 3303 Water Street, one of the first green roofs in the city, the owners of the building came to us for design help.

Our assignment was to create a 6,000-square-foot outdoor garden of an indoor/outdoor conference center that could suit different users and serve multiple functions. The elevated garden needed to function as a coworking and event space, but we could also not neglect what might be its more frequent use as a lush retreat where those working in the building could take a quiet break on a daily basis.

The most notable asset of the rooftop is a spectacular view of the United States Capitol. Although the clients leaned toward keeping the rooftop open and uninterrupted, we persuaded them that the view would be more dramatic if it were rationed. We also planned the inclusion of a pergola, to frame the vistas and to be a shelter from the sun during the warmer months.

When working atop a building, engineering inevitably becomes a fundamental consideration in the creation of any garden, and structural considerations dictate the quantity of soil the building can support. Here we were limited to an eight-inch-deep planting layer. Any trees would have to be placed directly on top of supporting columns.

Such a relatively shallow depth of soil could have been a severe limitation on our plant choices. Usually, green roof designers rely on a handful of repetitive, tried and true species such as sedums. Fortunately, in our previous work, we had identified a wide range of perennials, grasses, and even shrubs that would thrive in such conditions. In addition, we used high-density foam to lift the plantings, adding topographical definition to the space, without adding more weight. As a result, we were able to create an undulating, richly textured, and varied tapestry structured with *Rosa* 'Knockout,' *Cotoneaster salicifolius* 'Scarlet Leader' (willowleaf cotoneaster), and *Taxus baccata* 'Repandens' (English yew).

Ultimately, we organized the rooftop into two distinct spaces. We created a south terrace paved with limestone, centered on the view of the Capitol. The pergola, designed by Gensler, Washington, DC, was set on a floor with wooden decking that was more verdantly planted to offer a more intimate and sheltered retreat.

We used every dimension of the spaces for planting. Beds ran laterally while trellises climbed walls. Planters created outdoor 'rooms' and seating niches.

The challenge was to plan for a conference crowd of 200 people, while not neglecting the needs of the single individual. So, while considering how a group would circulate through the space, we had to also keep in mind the experience that one person in search of a quiet spot for a coffee break with a book might have. This made the design an interesting exercise in balancing the two spatial needs.

The paired terraces have proven very popular, and not just with human visitors. The two elevated gardens have become a mecca for birds seeking a haven in the city. This is an affirmation of our planting, a needed natural element in a city of built spaces, and a source of considerable entertainment for the office workers who use the garden.

RIGHT Without shelter, such an exposed rooftop space can be very hostile—windswept in winter, and under a pitiless summer sun. The lattice-roofed arbor provides protection from the elements. To ensure a sense of intimacy, we divided the space into two levels, with a 12-inch step-up from the more structured, limestone-paved lower level, to the cozier, wood-decked upper one. Planters frame and structure the spaces.

OVERLEAF LEFT To soften the architecture and enhance the garden-like effect, we worked with the architect to bring the greenery up the walls on elegant, though simple, trellises.

OVERLEAF RIGHT The shade of the trellises benefits the plants as well as the people, as proven by the luxuriant growth in the planters.

PAGES 256–257 Paired views reveal not just the seasonality of this garden—from late spring with its tapestry of blues, *Allium giganteum* (giant ornamental onion), *Nepeta racemosa* 'Walker's Low' (catmint), and *Salvia nemorosa* 'Mainacht' (wood sage), to the bold foliages of tropicals such as *Ipomoea batatas* (ornamental sweet potato) and other textural effects in high summer—but also how robustly the plants matured. The *Magnolia virginiana* (sweetbay magnolia), a sapling at the far rear, *left*, has become a stout young tree a couple of years later, *right*.

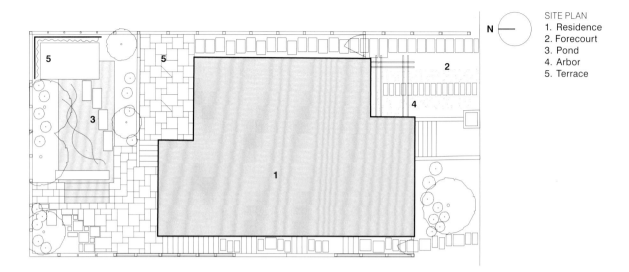

SITE PLAN
1. Residence
2. Forecourt
3. Pond
4. Arbor
5. Terrace

OPPOSITE Making the most of a small space, a large lily pool occupies almost the entire back yard. Designed as a self-sustaining ecosystem, its water spills down over three stone steps to aerate it so that the fish will find the oxygen they need.

The initial telephone call was irresistible. The prospective clients said that restoring their home had been a slow process, but they had known for more than eight years that it was OvS they wanted to turn their yard into a garden. Flying to the West Coast, we found a beautiful, yet still in progress, Arts & Crafts residence on a small, but promising, lot—and a client who was passionately engaged in every aspect of the design process.

The clients, both scientists, are very thoughtful people. She found a counterpoint to her very cerebral profession in her hands-on work with plants. Deeply rooted to her Dutch heritage, she sought a garden that would provide her and her husband with a respite from the demands of their professional lives. She also wanted a garden that was unique and extremely personal.

The client had a deep practical knowledge of plants, and what she didn't already know, she tirelessly researched. This led to many fruitful conversations between client and designer. The clients had even prepared sketches and a list of plants they wanted to include. The garden retreat focused primarily on the back yard, centered on a lily pool, which they wanted to be as large as possible.

So a large rectangular pond set slightly off-center, following the sloping grade, became the focus of the space. Fish, as well as water lilies and other aquatic and emergent plants, are interspersed among rectangular stepping stones hovering just above the water's surface, which lead to a wooden deck that extends out over the pond's northeast corner. Opposite the deck, three stone water steps create a cascade that descends to, and out over, the pond. While maximizing the water feature, we also

made the most of the green space. The rear garden, which, because of local codes had to be earthquake-proof, was leveled with a series of retaining walls, planted with cosmopolitan flora appropriate to the region, and fine-tuned to the taste of the clients. As the plantings were largely shaded by the house and the tall surrounding fences, the space became a garden of green hues. We created a tapestry by playing with textures, juxtaposing bold, large-leaved plants such as *Fatsia japonica* (Japanese aralia) and *Darmera peltata* (umbrella plant) with linear *Asplenium scolopendrium* (hart's tongue fern) and *Hakonechloa macra* (Japanese forest grass). Compact flowering trees and shrubs such as a *Stewartia sinensis* (Chinese stewartia) and a *Melianthus major* 'Purple Haze' (honey bush) provide structure and foliary color: The honey bush has purple-tinted leaves and those of the stewartia turn bright red in the fall.

We carried the planting from the horizontal into the vertical by bounding the garden on the northeast corner with expansive green walls. This was created by suspending felted material upon the fence in which a vegetative mosaic of plants could root. Such growth is encouraged by dripping moisture through a matrix from emitters on the top of the wall. The water comes from the pond, pre-enriched by the fish so that no fertilizer needed to be added. The plants, in turn, extract the nutrients from the water, optimizing their growth, helping to purify and cleanse it, restoring a natural, self-perpetuating cycle to the cityscape.

Every inch of the urban lot was carefully curated to exploit the amount of green and blue space. The garden is perfectly in tune with the clients, the environment, and the lovingly restored house that it surrounds.

RIGHT Accessible only via stepping stones placed over the pool's surface, the intricately detailed deck is banked by a rich complex of plants, to turn it into a private retreat from the surrounding cityscape.

OVERLEAF The clean lines and formality of the sandstone slabs lend a sculptural quality that provides a dramatic contrast to the ambient planting, in turn accentuating its lushness. Planting the same perennials in the green wall behind the deck as in the beds around the pool enabled us to fold the planted area visually up into a third dimension.

260

The desirable downtown site had for decades been occupied by a much-loved but threadbare public library. When EastBanc, a developer, bought the air rights over the existing building, it proposed a transformation that would benefit all parties by installing a state-of-the-art library on the ground floor of a new multi-floor condominium. Designed by TEN Arquitectos, a firm founded by the internationally acclaimed Mexican architect, Enrique Norten, the building was conceived as a series of ratcheting stacks of glass boxes, a concept that was not only visually interesting but which ensured that each unit would have a compelling view. It also created the opportunity to integrate the landscape and the building, another key element of Norten's design.

When we arrived in 2013, our brief was to create an array of landscapes that would serve as intimate counterpoints and complements to the architecture. We accomplished this in part by erasing the conventional distinction between indoor and outdoor spaces. New gardens around the exterior of the library floor provide patrons with attractive views and screen off the surrounding cityscape. We also leveraged the intimate interior courtyard garden, creating a shady glen of shrubs including *Fothergilla gardenii* (dwarf fothergilla) and *Ilex verticillata* 'Winter Gold' and 'Southern Gentleman' (winterberry hollies) that have been surrounded with perennial flowers and grasses and, to wake up the garden in spring, a host of bulbs: *Scilla siberica* (Siberian squill), *Narcissus* 'Weena' (daffodils), *Allium cernuum* (nodding onion), and *Allium sphaerocephalon* (drumstick allium).

We also planted a wall that continued from the courtyard into the lobby. Outside, on the courtyard stretch of the wall, *Hydrangea anomala* subsp. *petiolaris* (climbing hydrangea) clothes the concrete with green. On the inside, a green wall of plants was treated as a living mosaic. Assisted by Sempergreen, a nursery in Culpeper, Virginia,

which specializes in green roof and wall systems, we took a painterly approach to the design of the wall—dividing it into a grid of three-foot by three-foot squares. Each square of this grid was numbered and then translated into a series of pre-grown panels. When all the panels had grown in, they were hung on the corresponding spot on the wall to reproduce the original design in a pattern of ferns; *Adiantum pedatum* (northern maidenhair), *Asplenium antiquum* 'Victoria' (bird's nest), *Asplenium dimorphum* x *difforme* (Austral Gem fern), and *Cyrtomium falcatum* (Japanese holly), *Chlorophytum comosum* (spider plant), *Ficus repens* (climbing fig) and *Philodendron selloum* (tree philodendron) and *Philodendron hederaceum* (heartleaf philodendron), creating an instantly mature, vertical sheet of green.

The three-dimensional treatment of the design continued on the exterior. The stacked boxes of the structure provided a wealth of roof space on which to make elevated landscapes. Intensive green 'roofs' with a deeper layer of growing medium received a complex of compact shrub roses, perennials, grasses, and spring bulbs. Where the engineering dictated an extensive green roof with a lighter, shallower layer of growing medium, we planted a tapestry of mixed sedums in varying textures and colors.

Finally, to carry the green from the building out into the surrounding cityscape, we worked with the District of Columbia to place street trees around three sides of the building, setting four-and-a-half-inch caliper *Liquidambar styraciflua* 'Hapdell' (sweetgum) into sand-based structural soil that has been found to promote healthier rooting of urban trees and greater longevity. In the seven years since the trees were planted, this treatment has in fact promoted notably stronger, more vigorous growth, providing a substantial leafy canopy and interface between the street and the building.

OPPOSITE Enrique Norten conceived of The Westlight as a complex of box-like condominiums stacked over a ground-floor public library. Our role was to integrate the interior with the streetscape while also supplying amenities to the condominium owners.

RIGHT Support columns inside the glass exterior walls of the library create an abstract forest of stylized trunks. By running the plantings right up to the building on the outside, we supplied a green understory to this urban grove.

RIGHT The transparent glass walls of the building allowed us to blur the division between indoors and out. In the lobby of the residential area, an interior "living" green wall creates a visual echo and seamless transition.

RIGHT The engineering of the building dictated that different roof areas could support a variety of depths of growing media, ranging from a four-inch depth that could support only shallow-rooted, drought-tolerant sedums, *right*, to eight inches or even more, which could support perennials and shrubs. The rectangular planes of green were interwoven in a deliberate and architectural way.

The Martin Luther King, Jr., Library is not only the sole
library designed by Mies van der Rohe, but also the only
work by this giant of Modernist architecture in Washington,
DC. The redesign of the library's landscape gives a very
fair picture of the work with historic structures often
undertaken by the firm. These projects present a special
challenge that includes the requirement to create a fresh
landscape for contemporary users, while also respecting
the building's important historical context.

Intended to serve as the central library for the citywide
library system, the building was completed and opened to
the public in 1972, three years after the death of the
architect. Although greeted as a triumph at the time of its
opening, the library fell out of step with the public over the
following half century. A literal lack of transparency to a
landscape that included hidden corners had made it a
magnet for illicit activity. Also, a desire to green the original
skin-and-bones/less-is-more structure and make it more
environmentally friendly drove a reconceptualization of the
landscape design, an opportunity presented to OvS by the
Dutch architecture firm Mecanoo (Design Architect) and
Washington, DC's OTJ Architecs (Architect of Record).

Addressing the illicit activity began with installation of
improved architectural lighting both in and around the
exterior of the ground floor. At the same time, the public
area surrounding the building was reinvigorated and made
safer. Damaged pavers were removed and replaced, tree
grates were removed to make way for larger planting
areas, and a new generation of infill trees, a *Quercus rubra*
(red oak) and three *Ginkgo biloba* (maidenhair tree) were

installed to complete the streetscape. The amenity space
at the rear of the building was also rethought. Narrow and
sunken below grade, it was surrounded by masonry walls
and was a hidden and uninviting space. Expanded by the
removal of a garage ramp, sections of the wall were
removed and replaced with a transparent glass guardrail
so that the interior was no longer hidden from view. Built-in
wood amphitheater-style seating and the addition of tables
and chairs welcome users to enjoy the new cafe in the
midst of a verdant, planted backdrop.

A greater scope for creativity was the result of
converting the roof of the building to green space. This
serves the practical function of storm water management,
but is also a new venue for visitors. A new catering kitchen
and event space atop the building was capped with
a shallow green roof planted with sedums. All terraces,
planters, and guardrails were set back from the outer edge
of the building so that the view from the street would
remain unchanged.

The 14,900-square-foot area surrounding the addition
became a usable terrace. The western side of the roof was
planted with sedums, too, but on the eastern side, large
containers accommodate greater plant diversity, mid-Atlantic
natives, and adapted flora. These planters created three
themed gardens—a flower-filled native Pollinator Garden,
a Sensory Garden filled with aromatic herbs and slender
perennials and grasses that would move with the wind, and
a Seasonal Garden that would remain colorful from the first
spring bulbs to the russets and golds of grasses in the fall
and into winter.

RIGHT A view across
G Street NW shows the
newly renovated library's
two levels of green
roofs—one, extensive,
on top, and the other,
intensive, below, with
the new tree plantings
along the street.

RIGHT *Echinacea pallida* (pale purple coneflower) makes a strong statement, with its tall, dark seedheads in a late summer view of the Seasonal Garden. The lower white blossoms of *Allium cernuum* (nodding onion) provide a subtle counterpoint. The tawny drift of *Panicum virgatum* 'Heavy Metal' (switchgrass) adds a hint of the approaching change of season.

6

FARMS AND FIELDS

There is, of course, the difference in scale. Any design project begins with the clients and their program, with the designer determining how to furnish what the clients want while also marrying beauty, utility, and conservation. In this respect, our work on bigger properties such as a working farm or a large art park is similar in its fundamental core to our work on smaller residential projects.

But scaling up from a few acres or less to a matter of hundreds, or even thousands, brings with it certain complexities. A working property—a horse farm or a cattle ranch, for example, necessarily includes programs other than just the clients' desires—the needs and functions of the animals, whether they are farmyard animals or beloved saddle horses.

Nature also imposes a program. A small, residential property has its natural assets and challenges, but when these are magnified many times, the natural dynamics of the site become more powerful. We find ourselves dealing not only with a building lot, but with an ecosystem, or, in extreme cases, multiple ecosystems. The difference in scale also dictates designing with a larger, often more complex topography, with more intricate aspects of geology and hydrology. Each of these elements combine to provide a framework into which we fold land stewardship, conservation, and ecological health.

All of these programs must be integrated, like a series of transparent overlays placed one by one on top of each other over the base plan of the property. In designing a horse farm, we may begin by designing gardens around the residence, perhaps making the gardens more formal around the house and breaking them down more informally as we move out into the landscape. But there are also the horse barns and paddocks that need to be worked into the design, and these have to relate to each other in a workable fashion. Each piece requires a solution of its own that has to be right. All the pieces have to fit seamlessly with each other to make a whole.

Then there are the vistas. Residential properties may, and often do, boast views, but while these should be incorporated into the design, they are exterior to it. In a farm or ranch that stretches to the horizon, the vistas are intrinsic to the property and are a central element of the design process. On larger properties, it is essential to look not only at the earth but up to the sky as well. This can be especially true in more expansive, spread-out landscapes where the sky looms large. In the Big Sky country of Montana or the bush of Australia, and even on the flatter expanses of Michigan or Maryland's Eastern shore, the sky and the views to the horizon become a central element of the design. Whatever features are created in such a landscape have to be drawn with a bold hand. They must fit the expansive natural scale.

One useful rule-of-thumb inherited from our founders, Jim and Wolfgang, is to work with the proclivities of the land, to enhance its drama by accentuating its extremes. If it is naturally dry, go with that, and create a xeric composition. If the land is naturally wet, revel in that. Make the water the theme of the design. Celebrate the land for what it is.

Recognizing and acknowledging the natural in the design speaks to a particular strength of OvS' approach to farms and fields. We work with the potential of such working landscapes to make them not only beautiful and functional, but also as sustainable as possible. We have become very experienced over the years at tapping into expert advice. We seek to determine and incorporate the current best practices for managing that kind of landscape and that kind of usage, to make the project work not only for the present, but also to preserve and protect the land for the future.

RIGHT Once a 10,000-acre sheep station, the cattle ranch in New South Wales, Australia, is the part-time home of a returning client.

RIGHT Closer to the house, the pool complements the shape of the more-distant pond. A serpentine wall creates a graduated series of grass terraces from which to view the rolling topography, in particular the prominent hilltop, colloquially known as "The Lizard."

RIGHT Utah's Red Butte Garden, geologically unique and rugged, plays host to a high-altitude garden for all seasons. The landscape plane provides a canvas for abstract views of the distant jagged mountains. Autumn brings rich hues of warm oranges, reds, and browns, contrasting with the conifers and clusters of perennial seed heads.

TIPPET RISE ART CENTER FISHTAIL, MONTANA

OPPOSITE Though rugged, the landscape is also surprisingly fragile. The passage of cars or trucks, for instance, leaves traces in the grassland that remain visible for years. Our treatment of the landscape had to be sensitive and calculated to reduce such impacts.

OVERLEAF LEFT At 10,260 acres, Tippet Rise is an exceptionally expansive landscape, even by the standards of the American West. As part of our preparation, we asked the clients to list their favorite sculpture parks. All could be easily contained within Tippet Rise's boundaries.

OVERLEAF RIGHT Designing circulation to the destinations that the sculptors selected for their works within Tippet Rise was a complex task that included laying out paths for walking and bicycling, as well as for electrically powered vehicles designed to minimize disturbance to the landscape.

Vast spaces with a broad spread characterize this 10,260-acre expanse of Montana rangeland. The clients had a plan as bold as the landscape. They wanted to continue the property's century-old heritage as a working cattle and sheep ranch, while also establishing the Tippet Rise Art Center (TRAC) as a place where music, art, and nature are experienced simultaneously.

Our goal was to ensure that the design interventions worked with the land, rather than against it. Integrating the two uses of the land involved immersive exploration and study. We began with an in-depth benchmarking study that focused, in part, on a study of the visitor experience of other successful, large-scale sculpture parks worldwide. The study brought into focus one of the chief challenges of the project, humanizing the scale while maintaining the land's wild beauty. All the other comparable sculpture parks studied, although ample in their context, were easily dwarfed by the extent of Tippet Rise.

Coupled with this was the fact that although the land appeared rugged, it was in fact ecologically fragile. Set between the Beartooth Mountains to the south and higher plateaus to the north, it is an ecotone, an ecologically transitional area that is especially complex and rich in terms of flora and fauna. In addition to the herds of cattle and sheep, the ranch is home to mule deer, elk, coyotes, the occasional bear, and migrating sandhill cranes. The landscape is dry (less than 16 inches of precipitation per year), scarred by fire, windswept, and marked by wildly variable temperature fluctuations. The foothill grassland and short-grass prairie that covers the land is sensitive to disturbance, and unconsidered travel by vehicles is likely to leave long-lasting tracks. Worse, the heat of a vehicular exhaust system is more than enough to spark fires in the extremely arid grasslands.

Conceiving the control and circulation of visitors became central to the design process. The challenge only increased as artists began choosing sites to display their work across the ranch, with individual pieces often located miles apart. The difficulty of judging distances was increased by the horizontal nature of the landscape. Without any vertical reference points, distances become difficult to read. The team responded by exploring on foot, on bicycle, and in an electric vehicle, in order to gauge the ease and/or difficulty of navigating the varied terrain.

At the heart of TRAC, nestled along a creek and among a rough yet majestic Cottonwood hedgerow, is a collection of buildings, an outdoor performance space, and placed sculptures that serves as points of arrival and orientation. The Olivier Music Barn, designed by the Wyoming-based Gunnstock Timber Frames, seats 150 people for indoor performances, while the *Tiara*, an outdoor acoustic shell, designed by Arup Engineers, in New York, provides performance space, and *Xylem*, an outdoor pavilion, designed by the Berlin, Germany-based architect Diébédo Francis Kéré, is immersed in nature. Will's Shed, a dining facility, cottages for performers and sculptures by Patrick Dougherty and Mark di Suvero complete the tableau. The seemingly organic collection of buildings was carefully sited to maximize distant views, provide vistas, and leverage the topography to maximize universal accessibility.

The landscape, while blending with the surrounding environs, is intentionally restorative, revitalizing the Cottonwood hedgerow and optimizing it for both human and animal use. Stewardship, conservation, and sustainability are fundamental to Tippet Rise's mission. Elevated solar panels not only charge electric vehicles but provide shelters where visitors wait for transportation. Underneath the accessible parking area next to the Olivier Music Barn, we buried a 100,000-gallon cistern to collect rainwater and snowmelt—for flushing toilets and to irrigate the immediate landscape, keeping the grass greener and fire-resistant.

We never lost sight, however, of the traditional use of this land and the importance of stewardship. The Cottonwood Site was planted with especially nutritious and digestible grasses so that when the other rangeland was full of toxic *Toxicoscordion venenosum* (death camas) in the spring, the ewes and lambs can be pastured here. At the same time, we designed the area to be heavily planted with summer-blooming flowers that would make these meadows visually appealing during the summer arts season when the sheep had been moved to other rangelands.

Tippet Rise Art Center opened in 2016 to international media recognition and a continually sold-out schedule of concerts. Visitation surpassed initial estimates. On the Montana rangeland, art, music, and sustainable land stewardship co-exist as one.

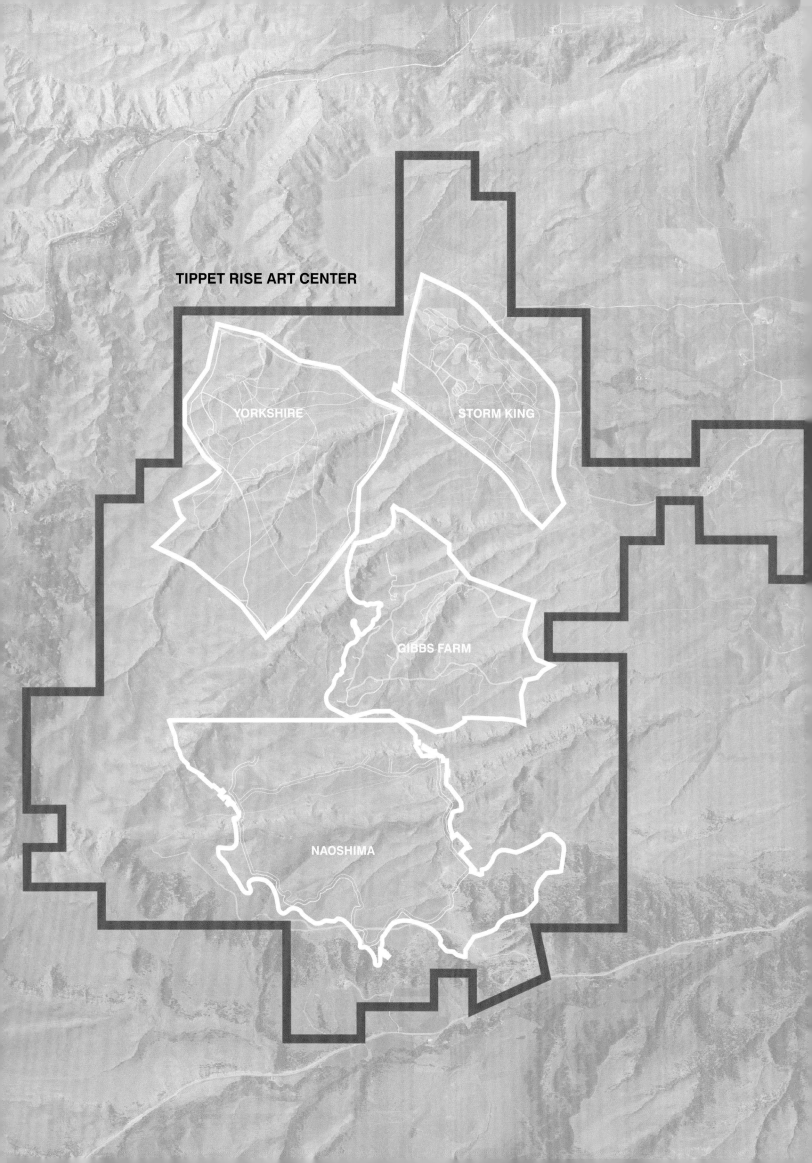

TIPPET RISE ART CENTER

YORKSHIRE

STORM KING

GIBBS FARM

NAOSHIMA

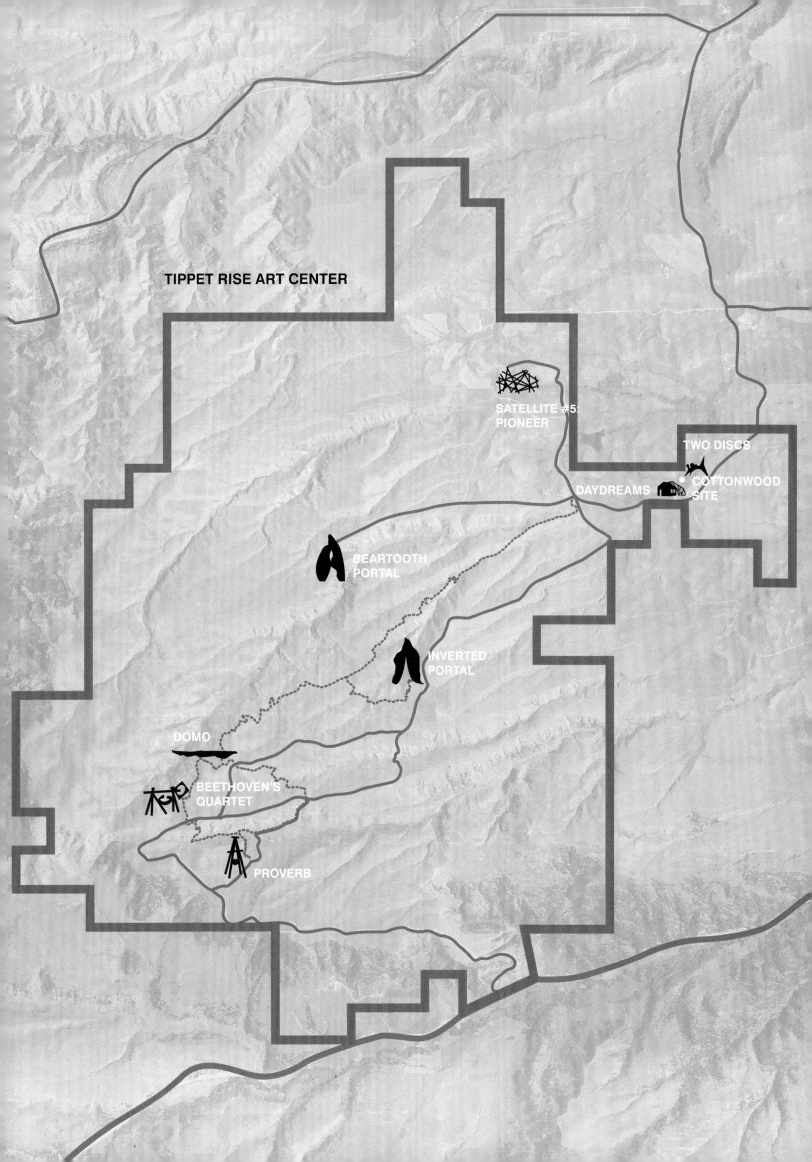

TIPPET RISE ART CENTER

SATELLITE #5:
PIONEER

TWO DISCS

DAYDREAMS   COTTONWOOD
                 SITE

BEARTOOTH
PORTAL

INVERTED
PORTAL

DOMO

BEETHOVEN'S
QUARTET

PROVERB

RIGHT Shallow soil, a dry climate (an average of 16 inches of precipitation annually) and periodic wildfires make this a landscape inhospitable to trees. The lack of vertical elements makes distances difficult to read, and increased the challenge of locating the sculptures. In general, each piece was settled into its own valley, to allow the sculpture to create its own world.

OVERLEAF LEFT Springtime, when the soil is moistened by a combination of snowmelt and seasonal rains, is lush. Sculptor Mark di Suvero's *Proverb* is at the rear.

OVERLEAF RIGHT The landscape is also home in spring to a rich variety of birds, such as sandhill cranes, as well as other wildlife, including bears and coyotes.

RIGHT Relics from the early settlers, inhabitants of a less technologically driven era, provide clues to working with, rather than against, the landscape: Dwellings historically built not on the windswept hilltops are nestled into protected slopes or valley bottoms.

RIGHT Poised on a gentle slope just above a cottonwood-lined creek, the Olivier Music Barn provides, not a statement, but rather a discovery for the incoming visitor. Modern materials meet traditional craftsmanship in this structure, which is timber framed inside, but clad in fireproof Corten steel outside.

OVERLEAF Two views illustrate how we collaborated with the landscape at the Cottonwood Site. Lacking vertical elements, the land is hard to gauge visually, confounding the eye, *top*. Stepping down the hillside above the creek, the Music Barn, Will's Shed (the dining pavilion), and the artist residences domesticate the site, *bottom*, providing a focus and a scale of measurement without compromising the view.

RIGHT **The Olivier Music Barn, itself a commanding presence in the landscape, is dwarfed by Tippet Rise's rolling topography and the nearby Beartooth Mountains.**

RIGHT African architect Diébédo Francis Kéré emphasizes sustainability in his work; he constructed a pavilion from timber reclaimed from lodge and ponderosa pines killed by the pine bark beetle. Called *Xylem*, the structure is derived in part from Kéré's memories of community gathering places in his native Burkina Faso. It is also an exploration of the organic forms found in the trees along the Cottonwood Site's creek. *Xylem* is the vascular tissue that forms the core of the trunks and draws water upward from the soil. We worked with Kéré to envelop the pavilion in a grove of *Populus tremuloides* (quaking aspen) and *Populus deltoides* (eastern cottonwood).

RIGHT To supplement the Music Barn, an outdoor music shell was built a short stroll away to provide a venue for outdoor audiences. Designed by the British firm Arup Engineers, the shell is wall-less and roofless, seemingly rudimentary, yet it reflects 90% of the concert sound back to the audience. Nestled into the landscape and surrounded by burgeoning *Populus tremuloides* (quaking aspen) trees, the *Tiara* is one of several outdoor performance spaces.

RIGHT Patrick Dougherty's sculpture, *Daydreams,* was based on one of the clients' memories of his mind wandering during his school days. Dougherty wrapped willow withies into twisting, flowing ropes that he then wove over and through a replica of a frontier-era schoolhouse.

RIGHT To take the musical performances farther afield from the Olivier Music Barn, *Domo* was created by Ensamble Studio in 2016 at the opposite corner of the ranch. Gravel was mounded and then swathed in plastic sheets to serve as a form for poured-in-place concrete. After the concrete cured, the gravel was dug away and the top of the resulting structure was covered with soil and planted with a native shortgrass prairie mix to root the open-air concert hall.

OVERLEAF LEFT The intent of Tippet Rise is to remove the arts from their high-culture housing and spread them into the landscape and life at large. Ensamble Studio's *Inverted Portal, top,* invites the visitor to enter fully into the view of the distant Beartooth Mountains. Installed at Tippet Rise in 2015, *Beethoven's Quartet* by Mark di Suvero, *bottom,* is massive and requires a monumental landscape to be displayed to full advantage. Mallets are provided to strike a tone from the stainless steel hanging element, which weighs 7,000 lbs.

OVERLEAF RIGHT A meditation on the (relatively) tiny tools we use to measure infinity, di Suvero's *Proverb* is absorbed effortlessly into the immensity of this landscape. Visitors and artworks co-exist seamlessly with the business of a working ranch at Tippet Rise.

RIGHT Montana's famous
Big Sky furnishes an
ideal, and spectacular,
backdrop for Stephen
Talasnik's *Satellite #5:
Pioneer*. Made of yellow
cedar and steel, this
50-foot-tall sculpture is
designed to accentuate
the contours of the
surrounding landscape.

OEHME, VAN SWEDEN PRINCIPALS

Rooted in a large, Irish-Catholic family from Connecticut, **SHEILA BRADY** is as much an artist as she is a landscape architect. From a young age, she has found beauty in the natural world and interpreted it through sketches, watercolors, and pastels. Her passion was translated into a Bachelor of Arts in Education and Fine Arts from George Washington University and a Master of Landscape Architecture from Harvard University's Graduate School of Design.

Sheila started working with OvS in 1988, where today she continues her artistic approach. Though New England always remains metaphorically close, Sheila has considered Arlington, Virginia, her home for over 30 years.

From an early age, **LISA DELPLACE** was fascinated by the inherent connection between people and the natural world. Raised in southeast Michigan, she cultivated a keen awareness of the region's geography and sensitive ecology, while developing a love of art and photography. Her curiosity fostered an ability to craft spaces that are geographically appropriate, ecologically sound, experientially rich, and artistically executed.

With a degree in Park Planning and Design from Michigan State University, a Master of Landscape Architecture from the University of Michigan, and Peace Corps service in Kenya, Africa, Lisa has worked for more than 30 years with OvS. She was appointed Chief Executive Officer in 2003.

Lisa lives in Washington, DC, with her husband Chris and their two latest boxer rescues: N'Rico and Mz. Pea.

ERIC GROFT is the second generation of his German-heritage Pennsylvania Dutch family to live off the farm. He grew up in the historic city of Lancaster, Pennsylvania, in a neighborhood between the red-brick market town and the farm fields.

After completing undergraduate studies at the Shippensburg University of Pennsylvania in Geography and Environmental Science, and a Master of Landscape Architecture at the University of Virginia, Eric landed at OvS in November of 1986. He has been with the firm ever since. Eric is widely recognized as an industry leader in ecological sensitivity, environmental and wetland restoration, and shoreline stabilization and revetment.

He lives in Annapolis, Maryland, with his two sons, Forest and Avery, and his Shepherd mix, Natty Boh.

FIRST GENERATION OvS was founded in Washington, DC, in 1975 by horticulturalist Wolfgang Oehme and landscape architect James van Sweden. Their partnership established a style known as the New American Garden, which is distinguished by a balance of horticultural exuberance and architectural craftsmanship. The New American Garden celebrates the seasonal splendor of the American meadow while promoting its inherent ecological and sustainable values.

SECOND GENERATION In 2001, the founding partners named Sheila Brady, FASLA; Lisa Delplace, FASLA; and Eric Groft, FASLA, as OvS' second generation of leadership. Under their guidance, the OvS style continues to evolve but remains driven by art, science, and emotional connections. The depth of the firm's 47 years of practice reflects OvS' ambition to enhance the urban experience, enrich communities, reimagine institutions, and inspire relationships between people and place.

THIRD GENERATION In keeping with van Sweden's belief that 'sustainability' applies just as much to the firm as it does to its work, OvS announced in 2022 the genesis of a third generation of leadership partners, comprised of six senior and long-time employees. Sara Downing, Stacilyn Feldman, Lili Herrera, Robert Johnson, Eva Lin, and Justin Maglione each bring diverse new energy and ideas to this firm and will help ensure that the OvS legacy continues well into the 21st century and moves "Further Beyond."

OEHME, VAN SWEDEN | OvS
800 G Street SE, Washington, DC, 20003 202 546 7575 ovsla.com

PROJECT CREDITS

ACKNOWLEDGMENTS

OPPOSITE In 2019, OvS embarked on an ambitious project: the renovation of the Rose Garden at the White House. The work was a close collaboration with First Lady Melania Trump, the Office of the Chief Usher of the White House, the Committee for the Preservation of the White House, the National Park Service, and fellow landscape architect Perry Guillot. The White House Rose Garden Landscape Report served as a framework on which to curate an outdoor experience transcendent of each administration and called for the return to the garden's original 1962 footprint as designed by Rachel "Bunny" Lambert Mellon during the Kennedy Administration. The renovated garden offers universal accessibility, a result of the new, perimeter limestone paving that frames the lawn. Critical upgrades to irrigation and drainage along with state-of-the-art electrical infrastructure for lighting and media technology were integrated into the design. The garden includes an additional 200 roses, chosen from species that will thrive in the space, a diverse palette of perennials, and a new variety of boxwood that delineates the parterres. The elements of the renovation were informed by cultural and historic precedents and reflect current thinking on sustainability, accessibility, and horticultural viability.

This book, the sixth in our series, is a tribute to the village that it takes to design, build, and maintain the gardens featured within its pages.

We could do none of this without our clients, whose vision, fortitude, and trust make our work possible. Of equal importance is our staff, who so diligently and tirelessly put in uncountable hours to sketch, assemble, draw, and execute the designs. To our design collaborators—the architects, interior designers, engineers, lighting-, and irrigation designers—each of you is truly steeped in the spirit of collaboration that is essential for a successful project. Finally, the vast array of contractors—general, landscape, and pool—along with the gardeners, masons, electricians, and teams of other talented specialists: You definitively realize our often audacious ideas and we are eternally grateful.

Prodigious thanks to those who directly helped to produce this book: Justin Maglione, Nathan Lucrisia, and all of the team at Pointed Leaf Press, especially the publisher, Suzanne Slesin, and the creative director, Frederico Farina. Our dear friend Charles Birnbaum begins the book with such thoughtful prose, Tom Christopher gives voice to our narrative, and all of the gifted photographers wholly capture the essence of our work. We are sincerely grateful for the time and effort you have provided us.

I want to extend my gratitude and admiration to my partners, Lisa Delplace and Eric Groft, and I would like to pay tribute to Jim van Sweden and Wolfgang Oehme for their endless mentorship. To Jim, for his immense business and design talents, and to Wolfgang for his extensive horticultural and planting design knowledge. I would like to offer a special dedication to my late husband John and my wonderful daughter Michaela.
—Sheila Brady

I must first acknowledge my family which is an unlimited source of support for all my endeavors. I thank Terry Brown, Bill Johnson, and Bob Grese, from the University of

Michigan, for introducing me to Jens Jensen, and giving me the confidence to design with nature. I am also eternally grateful to Elizabeth Meyer for introducing me to the work of Wolfgang Oehme and James van Sweden, who showed me how art, science, horticulture, and business combine to make a great firm. To Kris Jarantoski and the other extraordinary people at the Chicago Botanic Garden, for allowing me to practice my craft at such a fabulous institution. Sheila Brady and Eric Groft showed me how to make it all look easy! Martha Schwartz gives me laughter and reminds me how fragile our world is, and my international colleagues in Kenya, Nepal, Afghanistan, and the Ukraine helped me see landscape architecture through a culturally unique lens. Lastly, to my husband Chris McGahey, who is ever my compass, keeping me from getting lost along the way. Thank you.
—Lisa Delplace

It struck me, while participating in a 2015 edition of the National Building Museum's Spotlight on Design with my partners, that we, the second generation of firm principals, had survived both the transition of leadership from our founders and a global economic downturn. We had created a new body of diverse work that moved our founders' eponymous vision and unique approach in myriad and new directions and it was time to document these achievements. This book is that documentation.

To my partners, Lisa Delplace and Sheila Brady: We did it! I would like to pay tribute to my mentors, who have guided me through the most amazing journey I could imagine. My father, who introduced me to Ben Howland, who introduced me to Harry Porter at The University of Virginia, who started me on this journey. Wolfgang Oehme and James van Sweden changed my life forever and I think of you both every single day. Lastly, thank you to my sons, Forest and Avery. You have stuck by my side through thick and thin, dark and light, in sickness and in health. You are my guiding light and my inspiration to endure and achieve even greater heights.
—Eric Groft

INDEX

318

CAPTIONS

COVER The gardens at the American Museum & Gardens in Bath, United Kingdom, feature a distinctly American approach in a distinctly British setting. The bold palette includes *Allium giganteum* 'Summer Drummer' (giant ornamental onion), *Calamagrostis stricta* (slimstem reedgrass), and *Acanthus hungaricus* (bear's breeches).

FRONT ENDPAPERS A congregation of budding Allium in late spring reach for the moody sky in Bath, in the United Kingdom.

OPPOSITE HALF-TITLE PAGE Showcasing the beauty and diversity of the Northeastern United States, the Native Plant Garden at the New York Botanical Garden in The Bronx, New York, bursts with over 100,000 plants representing 454 species. The garden's sculptural water feature accommodates over 300,000 gallons and is a powerhouse of on-site storm water management.

PAGES 2–3 The Winding Walk at the American Museum weaves through bold sweeps of perennials that bloom from May to November, including *Agastache foeniculum* (anise hyssop) and *Verbena bonariensis* (purpletop vervain). The garden overlooks the Limpley Stoke Valley and the River Avon in Bath, United Kingdom.

OPPOSITE TITLE PAGE A private boardwalk bisects the privet hedge from perennial massings, connecting a house and its garden to the beach in Wainscott, New York.

PAGES 6–7 The plantings in an 18th-century farmstead garden in East Hampton, New York, blur the lines between the property and the surrounding rural landscape of fields and woods. *Tumbleweeds*, spherical sculptures by Aya Miyatake, dot the foreground of the arbored pool terrace.

PAGES 10–11 In Easton, Maryland, layers of *Pycnanthemum muticum* (mountain mint), *Panicum virgatum* (switchgrass), *Schizachyrium scoparium* (little bluestem), and *Rudbeckia maxima* (giant coneflower) give a brushstroke quality to the garden and draw the eye toward the water just beyond.

PAGE 316 Limestone pavers, generously spaced out at four inches and interplanted with *Thymus serpyllum* and *Mazus reptans*, zigzag through a garden on the East End of Long Island, New York.

PAGE 319 In 2015, OvS teamed up with Siebert & Rice, importers of fine Italian terra cotta, to design a signature line of plant containers known as OvS Organics.

OPPOSITE Spring in Westchester, New York, offers a multitude of verdant textures from hostas and *Cornus florida* (flowering dogwood) in a woodland garden.

BACK ENDPAPERS The grassed amphitheater at the American Museum & Gardens in Bath, United Kingdom. When not in use for events, the amphitheater is a favorite destination for children, who clamber up and down on the turf, while their parents recline on the sloped backs of the benches.

PHOTOGRAPHY CREDITS

Publisher / Editorial Director **SUZANNE SLESIN**
Creative Director **FREDERICO FARINA**
ISBN: 978-0-9777875-8-6
Library of Congress number: 2021922693
Printed in Spain / Second Edition